RAMAYANA
THE GAME OF LIFE

BOOK 5

RADIATE CONFIDENCE

Being Patient and Finding Success

SHUBHA VILAS

JAICO PUBLISHING HOUSE

Ahmedabad Bangalore Chennai
Delhi Hyderabad Kolkata Mumbai

Published by Jaico Publishing House
A-2 Jash Chambers, 7-A Sir Phirozshah Mehta Road
Fort, Mumbai - 400 001
jaicopub@jaicobooks.com
www.jaicobooks.com

RAMAYANA: THE GAME OF LIFE
Radiate Confidence – Book 5
ISBN 978-93-89305-12-8

First Jaico Impression: 2019
Third Jaico Impression: 2024
Fourth Jaico Impression (New Cover): 2025

Page design and layout: R. Ajith Kumar, Delhi

Printed by
Thomson Press India Limited, New Delhi

Acknowledgments

Walking through life, I have always seen myself as a student, surrounded by teachers who have touched and enhanced my life immensely. I would like to express my heartfelt gratitude for all that I have been fortunate enough to learn from them.

To name all of them here would be impossible; however, some of the most prominent teachers in my life have been: H.D.G. A.C. Bhaktivedanta Swami Srila Prabhupada, the founder Acarya of the Hare Krsna Movement and H.H. Radhanath Swami, the author of the international bestseller *The Journey Home – Autobiography of An American Swami.*

I am indebted to Valmiki muni, the author of the *Ramayana*. And Kamba muni, who further enriched the flavor of the original with his amazing poetry. And to Tulsidasji, whose analogies bring out deeper aspects of this epic. I have learnt a lot about the intricacies of the Ramayana from Sri Velukkudi Krishnan Swami and K.S. Narayanacharya, Sri Ramkumar Kinkarji, C. Sita Ramamurti and Sri S. Appalacharyulu. I would also like to appreciate all those who have worked on the website – www.valmikiramayan.net – to make the epic accessible to the world.

My special gratitude to Dr. Shrilekha Hada, for her tireless zeal and invaluable inputs in developing every aspect of the book. She has become an integral part of this series.

I personally owe a million thanks to Meera Menon, whose meticulousness shows through in every sentence of this book, whose thought-provoking enquiries have helped me go deeper into the *Ramayana*.

A monumental venture like this wouldn't be possible without constant encouragement from my friends. Particularly, Shadbhuj, Radeshlal, Raas Gopal, Raja Gopal and Nitin Chavan who have supported me in more ways than can be penned. I offer my gratitude hugs to them celebrating the joy of true friendship.

Probably the greatest inspiration has come from the thousands of readers who have enthusiastically written and spoken to me about their appreciation for these books and the life-transformation it has brought in their lives. I consider their wishes to be my primary motivation to keep writing.

And of course, my warm thanks to the entire team of Jaico, especially Akash Shah, Aadya Jha and Nita Satikuwar– their intense efforts and sincere dedication is visible on every page of the book. This book has been a memorable journey with so much contemplation going into making the series more accessible to the world. This journey has been about not only working on a book but also bonding deeply with the Jaico family. I am truly inspired and encouraged to continue this venture in making *Ramayana* everyone's life companion with their support.

Author's Note

Ramayana – The Game of Life series presents an authentic rendition of the *Ramayana* in an absolutely modern and riveting manner. This book promises to enlighten loyalists and entertain modernists. Interspersing the story of the *Ramayana* with thought-provoking contemporary life lessons, the series guarantees satisfaction – a volume that can prove to be a lifelong companion. As you flip the pages, one thought is sure to cross your mind: never has the Ramayana been so applicable to my life!

The book series, while holding Valmiki muni's *Ramayana* as a lighthouse, sensitively weaves in analogies and poetic ornamentation from the *Kamba Ramayana* and Tulsi Das' *Ramcharitmanas*. In addition, the series also brings in folk tales called Loka Pramana that are in philosophical alignment with Valmiki's *Ramayana*. These folk tales bring in background stories that enhance the understanding of the main story as well as its various characters and their moods. Without the knowledge of these tales, the original story would be much less dramatic and comprehensible. Moreover, the series also provides deep insights from the great acharyas who have studied the *Ramayana* thoroughly. Even if it is filled with so many elements, I have made sure that modern readers do not find it inapplicable or irrelevant in their personal life. This series shows readers how these epics have immediate relevance in our life, if presented properly and understood deeply.

Of course, I would like to state here that I have taken some creative liberties to keep the narration riveting and gripping. But rest assured, these creative liberties are minimal and do not, in any way, impede or supersede the original author's work or the divinity of the epic and its characters. If anything, the creative liberties enhance the joy of reading this great work of literature.

Over the last few years, I have presented a series of seminars based on *Ramayana –The Game of Life*, where I expand on the innumerable life lessons presented in the books with a lot of practical examples and anecdotes. These seminars have made the book even more user-friendly and relevant to the thousands who have heard them. These seminars are freely available on YouTube.

Radiate Confidence essentially expounds the *Sundara Kanda* of the *Ramayana*. This is the most sought after and popular section of the epic. Many people prefer to read and re-read only this section. This is the most thrilling book of the entire series as it talks about the beginning of Hanuman's heroic exploits. Every 'Kanda' or section of the *Ramayana* spans many months or, in some cases, many years. The *Bala Kanda* covers a period of almost 13 years, the *Ayodhya Kanda*, almost a year, the *Aranya Kanda*, stretches over roughly 13 years, while the *Kishkinda Kanda* describes a period of a little over two months. But the *Sundara Kanda*, the fifth book in the *Game of Life* series, covers just five days; and more than three-quarters of the book covers a two-day period when Hanuman leapt to Lanka.

Every character is a hero in his or her own right and has the power to arrest the attention of the reader in different ways, at multiple levels in various situations. The reader will be introduced to many new characters who will enhance their understanding of life and human psychology. This book is about Hanuman learning the art of "being patient and finding success," as the subtitle suggests. Through the story of Hanuman, readers are allowed to explore their own journey and learn how to deal with obstacles on their path to success.

CONTENTS

Chapter 1

Flight Across the Wild Waters

between the devil and the deep sea

The energy levels had all but flatlined, but enthusiasm was at its peak. The excruciating month-long search mission had sapped every ounce of strength they had, but a newfound hope had lifted their spirits and rejuvenated them. As the thousands of *vanaras* scampered through the thick woods, they applauded each other with loud hoots and shouts. Raucous cries echoed all around, and all the faces lit up with exuberant smiles.[1]

Then suddenly, the loud crack of thunder startled the power-packed army to a screeching halt. The bewildering boom was all it took to silence the rapturous troop. The sound resembled the rumble of countless battle chariots. Or was it like the roar of thousands of beasts together?

---

[1] When ordinary people choose to divorce Hope during difficulties, extraordinary people choose to marry her.

When married in the season of emergency, Hope gives birth to success in the season of normalcy.

As the army stood frozen at the outskirts of the forest, their breathing became heavier – thick air gushing in and out of their noses and mouths like the giant waves of the enormous ocean sprawled out in front of them. The *vanara*s exchanged anxious glances, as the nervous army edged its way toward its biggest obstacle yet: the colossal ocean.

The rogue waves seemed to dare them on. The wild breakers kept lashing the coast time and again, forcing the spirit-battered *vanara* army to step back. The waters spread far beyond their range of vision. Although several stretches appeared very still, the *vanara*s knew those tranquil waters were cradling the ocean's deepest rage. Conquering this surging monster seemed impossible.[2]

One by one, the *vanara* soldiers dropped to their knees, defeated and demoralized. Angad, the chief of the southern search party, stood up to motivate his men. It was his duty and the need of the hour. But the roaring waters drowned out the positive vibes of his lofty speech and bullied the army into silent submission. The long silences transitioned into sleep, and sleep dragged in nightmares of watery graves.[3]

Angad woke up early and persevered with his motivational talk. Eventually, he goaded his men to reveal their personal best leaping statistics. He figured that would not only lighten up the tension but also help find the one who could leap all the way across the ocean.

---

[2] In autumn, most cry for the falling leaves, but those strongly rooted in knowledge smile at the sight of sturdy roots.

Below every sign of despondency is a hidden sign of hope.

[3] Words of inspiration lose power when addressed to a despondent mind that rumbles negativity.

The record disclosure (and bragging) began with one sheepish *vanara* admitting that he could jump only a mile. That confession motivated some more to speak up. One by one, the *vanaras* started declaring their best, until one stood up and said, "Five hundred miles. I could leap as far as five hundred miles in one go." Everyone turned toward the leader Angad. Surely, he could outdo that. "I could easily do eight hundred," Angad confirmed. The beach erupted with rousing cheers, and the *vanaras* began to dance with joy. Now with that said, the target destination, Lanka, was within reach. It was exactly eight hundred miles across the ocean! On seeing this sudden surge of energy among the soldiers, Angad realized the enormity of his responsibility. So he cautioned his army, "...but I am not confident I will be able to return."[4]

The "but" had dragged them down just as soon as the "eight hundred" had lifted them up. Before Angad could even finish his sentence, everyone had slumped back into the sand. All the *vanaras* pinned his lack of confidence to faltering energy and ability. But the wise old Jambavan knew better. He knew that Angad's skepticism about returning had nothing to do with fear of failure. In fact, it was because of an entirely different kind of fear – the kind no leader would dare to share with his subordinates or admit to himself.[5] It was the kind of fear only a trained eye such as Jambavan's could spot.

Angad wasn't scared of leaping into and from the land beyond the ocean. Instead, he was afraid of falling right into temptation. As

---

[4] Whether it is the journey of life or a journey in life, having a return ticket is very important. More important than planning to take a risk is planning to return to safety.

[5] A weakness that you don't share with anyone is a weakness that you shudder to admit to yourself.

the son of Vali, succumbing to temptation was in Angad's blood. He knew Lanka was a place of illusion and desire. He wasn't sure if he could focus on the mission amid so many desirable distractions. Besides, he was unsure if being exposed to the razzle-dazzle would even make him want to leave. Angad and Jambavan exchanged glances. While the leader chose not to explain, the wise one decided not to reveal.[6]

Instead, Jambavan thought it best to speak about his own strengths. "Back in the day, I could do so much. But that's all in the past now. Thanks to this frail old frame, I can't even hop over a tiny puddle now, let alone leap across the eight hundred-mile ocean!"[7]

Jambavan turned around, searching for a ray of hope among the listless faces. Soon his eyes rested on the one who hadn't yet declared his leap figures. He had instead chosen a quiet spot for himself and decided against partaking in the pointless discussion. He sat on a rock facing the ocean, his eyes closed in meditation.

Jambavan walked up to the lone warrior, put his arm around his chiseled shoulder, and sat next to him. No words were exchanged for a while – the awkward silence shattered only by the sound of the waves curling over their feet and rushing back to the horizon. It seemed almost as if the ocean was luring them into a challenge.

---

[6] While ordinary people focus on abilities, leaders focus on mindsets. While the monkey army was focusing on Angad's ability, Jambavan focused on his mindset.

While ordinary people focus on what everyone can see, a leader focuses on what no one can see.

[7] Jambavan speaks about what he could do in the past, and Angad speaks about what he can do in the future. Between past glories and future anxieties, the present loses hope.

Jambavan knew it was about time they took up that challenge. So he stood up to face the sinewy warrior, his eyes surveying this beacon of hope. He chose his words carefully. "Hanuman, you are the son of Vayu. Do you not remember shrinking the distance between the earth and the heavens to micro moments? Do you not remember as an infant seeking to catch the sun, mistaking it for a ripe fruit? Do you not remember swallowing the sun and casting Rahu into your mouth because he was about to eclipse the sun? The universe itself will never forget the day, for the king of the heavens had to intervene to undo the catastrophe your innocent hunger had caused. His thunderbolt had not only smashed your chin, but also hit your father's heart. The subsequent tumble could not crush your enthusiasm; instead, it embellished you with blessings from many divine beings. You arose from the fall a much stronger and more vibrant entity."

Jambavan's words spurred the silent hero. His eyes began to sparkle. The more he heard about his exploits, the brighter his eyes shone.[8]

The crestfallen *vanaras* who had been sitting with their heads buried in their hands perked their ears and looked up at the two warriors and exchanged glances. There was hope, after all.

Jambavan went on. "You are Hanuman, the son of the wind god, the very wind that carries the breath of life. So, breathe life into our hopeless souls by storming into the land where Sita is captive.

---

[8] When a leader plants the seed of encouragement in one's mind, it grows into a tree of hope for many minds.

Jambavan encouraged Hanuman, who became the symbol of hope for millions.

Behind every ship that surges ahead is a gust of wind. Behind every hero who succeeds are a thousand whispers of encouragement.

Uthishta, Hanuman! Rise, Hanuman! If you could touch the sun with just one jump, surely, the ocean is a tiny puddle for you. Cross these rough waters and deliver us from this hopelessness.[9]

Hanuman was charged. Jambavan's words had struck a deep chord. Something he had long forgotten came back to him. He rose slowly, stretching his limbs.

Watching him, the *vanara*s straightened up, too. Hanuman's arms seemed to extend all the way up to the sky. "RAAAMAAAA." He cried out to his Lord and Master. As the intensity of his full-throated call increased, so did the size of his body. Hanuman's body began swelling up with the strength and power of Rama. Within moments, Hanuman had become this colossal being swatting clouds with his long tail. He pumped up his chest and let out a loud roar that ripped through the vicinity. His gaping mouth seemed like a mighty lion's den. The *vanara*s were thrilled with this transformation. They had experienced such low levels of motivation that Hanuman, who was now looming large, seemed like the only one who could elevate hope and infuse courage in them.

Their friend was now this ever-growing behemoth figure. Every muscle in his body had expanded to extraordinary proportions. He was now ten times his size. It was unlike anything the *vanara*s had seen before. As they watched, Hanuman continued to invoke Rama incessantly with his eyes closed. By the time he opened his eyes, he was fifty times his size.

Hanuman was now mission ready. His eyes darted across the surroundings. He had spotted his launch pad – the tall and mighty

---

[9] Reminders of past successes serve as the inspiration for future challenges.

Mahendra mountain. Three furtive leaps, and he was at the summit. As he stood on the peak scanning the vast ocean, it seemed as if there was one mountain atop another. To some, it appeared as if the Mandara mountain stood on the back of Kurmadev, the tortoise incarnation of Lord Vishnu. Hanuman's shadow alone was almost fifty *yojanas* long. The *vanaras* felt tiny in comparison.[10]

glorious take-off

"Yes, I can do anything! Like my father, I can reach any corner of the universe and return in a moment. I can leap across all the oceans at once. I can disperse the clouds in the sky and dry up the oceans. I will reach Lanka in one jump and find Sita there. If I can't find Her, then I will uproot Lanka and carry back the isle for us to search thoroughly. I can snatch the nectar of immortality right out of Indra's hands. I can do anything in the service of Lord Rama. I am unstoppable. Lord Rama does not need to take the trouble of going to Lanka. I will crush Ravana with my thumb and carry Sita back from Lanka."

The *vanaras* began to hoot and shout and started to gather around Jambavan. As the wise old warrior saw the prancing *vanaras* looking up at Hanuman all awe-struck, he said, "Go, Hanuman. Leap into the isle across the ocean and find Sita. Remember our lives depend on you. We will be glued to this spot and fast until your return. Our prayers are with you."[11]

---

[10] The birth of a hero always takes place on a mountain of challenges and not in the valleys of comforts.

[11] The pride of a teacher is in seeing the transformation of a student.

Hanuman folded his palms and bowed to his teacher Surya, the sun god. He then offered his respects to Indra, the god of the heavens, then Lord Brahma, the creator, and finally, he turned to his father, Vayu, the wind god. Then, turning south, he glared at the raging waters and the rough waves teasing him.[12]

From the beach, Hanuman was quite a vision standing atop the summit. Red, blue, black, white, green and yellow rocks were scattered all over the slopes. Everyone had heard and could now imagine the snakes of various sizes and shapes that slithered around the boulders on which Yakshas, Kinnaras and Gandharvas visiting the mountain with their consorts sat and made merry. However, little did they realize that this peaceful mountain would soon enough become the hub of extreme action.

From a distance, the ascetics, Vidyadharas, Siddhas, Charanas and other awestruck celestial beings watched the colossal wonder-*vanara* prepare for the impossible with his eyes shut. Confidence, strength, faith and determination reflected off his poised frame.[13]

Hanuman kneeled on all fours, placed his palms on the mountain floor, brought his right foot forward between his hands, stretched his right leg forward, with his left leg and coiled his tail behind him, before finally digging his feet to the ground to prepare for the lunge. As he took position, he stretched and slapped his muscles to

---

[12] Humility is born out of dependence, dependence out of appreciation, and appreciation out of respect, but respect is birthed in a heart free of pride.

[13] Before Hanuman made his jump, Valmiki *muni* described him in three adjectives. He called him *Parvathasankaasah*, meaning like a mountain, alluding to his strength; *Maaruthathmajah*, meaning the son of Vayu, pointing to his capacity to fly like the wind; and *Mahaavegah*, meaning one with great speed, referring to his ability to leap across the ocean.

charge himself, vigorously shook the hair on his body and let out an earsplitting roar that rumbled like storm clouds. He then crouched and curled his toes, arched his neck and looked skyward, took a deep breath, pressed his ears against his head and transferred all his strength and power onto his ankles. He then tightly coiled his tail into his back, released it with a sudden thwack and skyrocketed upward. While the tail-strike blasted the mountain rocks into smithereens, the immense pressure of the lift-off sucked in all the trees, plants and animals in the vicinity.

The pressure was so high that the leaves, flowers and fruits of the trees were ruffled and jolted off the naked branches. Millions of flowers, leaves and fruits rained on the *vanara*s standing by the ocean below the mountain. Soon, the entire coast and parts of the ocean were strewn with plants, trees and animals that had fallen off Hanuman's blazing trail once the pressure normalized.

From afar, the ascetics had watched the mountain tremble under the sudden immeasurable weight and force. The fragile blossoms on every tree on the slopes were startled off their stems. One moment the mountain was resplendent with multicolored rocks and pebbles, the next it was a flower carpet. The rammed mountain began to spew streaks of liquid gold, silver and antimony, shoot out sulfur boulders and eject horrified and howling beasts and humans out of their caves. Animal cries echoed across the land.[14]

The reverberations woke the venomous snakes from their slumber. They sprung out of their burrows with their hoods fanned out, hissing flames from their forked tongues. Dazed and disoriented

[14] Beauty is often irksome from proximity. To appreciate the beauty of life, one has to zoom out and view it from a distance.

by the chaos, the reptiles started to dig their fangs into the rocks. The poison was so potent that even the medicinal herbs on the slopes could not neutralize it. Instead, it oxidized the rock minerals, sparking a massive wildfire. The columns of smoke seemed like the mountain's incense offering to Hanuman.

The commotion unsettled all creatures on the mountain. *What's going on? Is it a demon attack?* No one seemed to have a clue, but everyone wanted to escape whatever it was.

The ascetics tumbled out of their caves and jumped off the rocks they were seated on. The Vidyadharas – their necks adorned with red flower garlands, their bodies smeared with red sandalwood paste and their restless eyes red and tipsy from a night of revelry – dragged themselves out of their cozy dens and escaped skyward with their women in tow, leaving behind them as litter their golden jugs of fine wine and shiny plates of exotic meals.

"Did you see that?" A *vanara* asked, his eyes still riveted on Hanuman, who was now only a speck in the sky. "That was powerful yet beautiful."

Another agreed. "It seemed like the flora and fauna on the mountain were seeing a dear one off on a long, arduous journey. Almost as if the plants and animals on the mountain had accompanied Hanuman up to a certain distance, as one would a loved one."

Yet another *vanara* said, "The trees now resemble soldiers silently following their king!"

"Look at the ocean now! So many flowers in so many hues – the waters resemble the night sky filled with twinkling stars." A poetic *vanara* commented.

Seeing everyone lose focus on Hanuman's flight, an inspired *vanara* spoke. "Forget the fallen ones; look at the one that has risen! With his arms spread out ahead of him, he is like a five-headed snake emerging from behind a mountain peak. Look at his face, glowing like the twilight sun. Those brilliant eyes are gleaming like the full moon. See his dazzling teeth impale even lightning. His intellect is as robust as his body. Even the wind slapping his muscular armpits sounds like thunder. His strong tail resembles the tough pillar erected for the worship of Indra. Look at Hanuman blazing through the sky like a meteor shooting across the galaxy."

The excited *vanara*s broke into a resounding applause, celebrating the greatness of their wonderful friend. Amid the enormity of this momentous occasion, one thought soared high above all the others: Hanuman's modesty. In all these years the *vanara*s had known him, Hanuman had managed to conceal his greatness and live a simple life among them, never once showing off through words or actions. His humility far outshone his heroism.[15]

Hanuman seemed like a boat sailing in the wind; his long shadow sprawled across the waters like a dense cloud. The sheer force of Hanuman zipping over the ocean caused the waters to part right down the middle into two tall, deep waves. The parting was so deep that it exposed the floor, making the aquatic creatures feel naked and unclothed.

---

[15] The greatness of great people is that they humbly hide their greatness.

The greatness of simple people is that they simply celebrate the greatness of great people.

This shows that simple people are simply great, and great people are humbly great.

Hanuman would disappear into and appear out of the large clouds, almost like the peeping moon. Sea serpents were petrified, assuming that their enemy Garuda was flying past. The Gandharvas, Apsaras, Devatas and the Danavas showered fragrant flowers on Hanuman. The sages standing atop the far-flung mountain wove verses to describe the majestic scene. The birds and the Gandharvas set their heartfelt verses to music. To make his journey comfortable, the harsh sun dimmed its glare and the wild wind hushed into a pleasant breeze.[16]

When all his brothers were toning down to facilitate Hanuman's mission, Varuna, god of the oceans, wondered how he could contribute. Thus far, he had only been an obstacle to finding Sita. He now wanted to change that and be of help. After all, didn't King Sagara of the Ikshvaku dynasty, to which Lord Rama belongs, create him? The ideal way of expressing gratitude would have been by being this large watery barrier and stopping Ravana from whisking away Sita. Back then, however, deep terror had choked him and rendered him inactive. A god-sent opportunity to assist the assistant of the descendent of his creator had fallen right into Varuna's lap, and he didn't want to miss this second chance. He assumed a weary traveler needed a good nap. So he summoned the

---

[16] In Hanuman's expedition, every element of nature is used in the service of Lord Rama.

By jumping over the ocean, he used the water element.

As son of Vayu, he used the air element.

By blazing across the sky, he used the ether element.

By meeting Sita who was also called Bhumisuta (one born from the earth), he worshipped the earth element.

By setting fire to Lanka, he used the fire element.

services of the golden Mainak, the mountain of comforts, which lulled to sleep anyone setting foot on it. The mountain's precious gift was many days of sound sleep. Varuna felt that during this long eight-hundred-mile journey to Lanka, a good rest would be a welcome break for Hanuman.[17]

Varuna spoke to the mountain. "O Mainak, do you remember how I saved you from the wrath of Indra? If you remember and are grateful for the shelter that I provided you for all these years, then it is time to reciprocate by helping me express my gratitude to someone who created me."[18]

As Mainak stood there obediently, his palms folded, Varuna continued. "I do not want you to move from your position because you are covering the entrance to the *patalalokas*. The *asuras* have been waiting for a chance to open the portal to the *patalalokas* to gain easy access to the earth. Stay fixed and expand your dimensions. Rise high enough to be seen on the surface of the waters. As you grow, you will find coming your way the mighty Hanuman, who is on a mission for Lord Rama. Offer him your best services and make him happy. That's all I expect.[19]

---

[17] A single expression of gratitude is worth more than a million secret appreciations.

[18] The gratitude chain broken by the hammer of selfishness has to be soldered by a welding machine called reminder.

[19] The only way to find happiness is to give happiness.

When you project happiness into another's life, happiness reflects back into your life.

obstacle one: wingless mountain

Suddenly the blue sky was a shade of resplendent gold. Hanuman was astonished by the sudden change in hue. Piercing out of the deep ocean, right in the middle of the water surface, was a fascinating golden mountain. Hanuman was flying at very high speed and did not manage to slow down on time, and his barrel chest collided with the highest peak. The intense impact shook the mountain and pushed it aside by a considerable distance. Hanuman halted his momentum and pivoted to take a good look at the golden mountain that obstructed him.

It was gorgeous, with flowering trees and fruit trees, picturesque parks and shimmering peaks with palaces. Fresh water lakes dotted the mountain that arose from the salty ocean floor. The luster of the golden mountain was comparable to a hundred brilliant suns. Attractive Kinnara men and women sat in the parks and along the lakes, indulging in song and dance. Standing with folded hands atop the highest peak was an effulgent personality. The golden aura of the mountain seemed to emanate from his body. He was looking at Hanuman with deep veneration.

Hanuman wasn't impressed. He was hardly a fraction into his eight-hundred-mile journey, and this obstacle was the last thing he needed. It surely looked important and impressive, but it was a barrier, nonetheless. Hanuman offered a reluctant yet polite half-smile. Mainak began eulogizing Hanuman's greatness and showering the flying hero with praise. "What you have set out to accomplish is beyond anyone's imagination. Every hero needs a good rest to achieve success. I am Mainak, and I am here to provide you with a much-needed break. To make this huge jump after months of arduous search across the length and breadth of the land must have exhausted you. I am equipped with every comfort ideal to rejuvenate and invigorate a tired body. Just surrender yourself for a few hours, and I assure you of complete rejuvenation and much more strength for your onward journey.[20]

Varuna is so grateful to the ancestors of Lord Rama who created him that he wants to reciprocate by showing kindness upon anyone connected to that dynasty. You are the foremost of Lord Rama's associates, and Varuna wants me to offer you a special treat. Gratitude needs to be expressed through action. Please allow, my master, to show his reciprocation to the Raghuvamsha by serving you during your service to them.

But I have a more personal and important reason. That alone is enough for me to serve you eternally, not just this once. Many years ago, every mountain in this world had wings and could fly freely to wherever they wished. Some of the mountains were so powerful that they could compete with Garuda and even Vayu in speed. Because of one or two freak accidents, all living things on earth developed a fear that the indiscriminate landing of the flying mountains put their lives in danger. They prayed to the *devas*, who promised to rectify the situation immediately. Instead of setting proper rules for flying and landing, Indra's solution was to chop off the wings of every mountain and make them immobile and harmless. When he finally came to amputate me, your father Vayu came to my rescue. To stop Indra from hitting me, he blew a mighty breath of wind that dislodged me from the path of the thunderbolt and pushed me into the ocean bed. Varuna agreed to shelter me. By the grace of the wind and water gods, my wings were saved from destruction. Varuna had a vested interest. He uses me to close the portal to the *patalaloka*.

---

[20] Obstacles often come disguised as beautiful aids.

But your father is just like you – without any agenda. Now is my chance to reciprocate your father's kindness by showing you small acts of kindness. By worshipping the son, I worship the father.[21]

Our culture teaches us to worship even an ordinary guest as god, but you are no ordinary guest. Everyone you are connected to is worthy of worship; therefore, you are worthy of worship. Even if we do not consider your greatness, there are so many reasons to worship you. If you add to that even a fraction of your greatness, it gives limitless reasons to serve you right now. Please come and enjoy the fruits and flowers here. Relish the nectarine waters and refreshing fragrant breezes. Let me take care of your fatigue and rejuvenate your body. Surrender yourself to this mountain and allow the pleasure treatment to help you experience the rejuvenation of your body."

After listening to Mainak patiently, Hanuman spoke his mind. "Just as you have an obligation to reciprocate, I have a duty to perform. Your obligation is not time bound, but my duty is. Every moment here is a moment of duty neglected. I will receive your thankfulness by simply touching you. Please understand that my father appreciates your love, your desire to serve and your genuine gratitude. Allow me to go ahead on my mission for my Master now."

Even before Mainak could utter a response, Hanuman touched the golden mountain and flew away. He not only accepted Mainak's offer but also did not waste any time reveling in comfort and neglecting

---

[21] Leaders insensitive to some and sensitive to others are actually sensitive about holding onto their positions and insensitive about carrying out their roles.

his duties. He had been sensitive to Mainak's feelings, yet he was alert enough about his duty in order not to allow the lure of comfort to derail it.

Hanuman had overcome the second obstacle. The first was gross, and the second was subtle. The first was the ocean, and the second was comfort. The first was tough, and the second was sensitive. The first needed external power, and the second needed internal alertness. The first needed ability, and the second needed absolute focus on the goal.[22]

No sooner than Hanuman was out of sight, Indra appeared to Mainak. He hadn't seen the golden mountain in ages. Varuna, the ocean god, was his protector, which meant Indra could not clip off his wings as he had for the other mountains. Mainak started to tremble. Just as he began regretting his foolish decision of leaving the protection of the ocean bed, Indra folded his hands and offered his respects to him. "You have done very well by offering to serve Hanuman who is on a mission in the service of Lord Rama. I am extremely pleased with you, Mainak. From now on, you will have no reason to fear me. This one act of service has absolved you of all your arrogance and pride."[23]

---

[22] The one sensitive to others' needs and inattentive to one's own is *selfless*.

The one insensitive to others' needs and attentive to one's own is *selfish*.

The one sensitive to others' needs and attentive to one's own is *wisely compassionate*.

[23] Just as one small spark can burn down mountains of camphor, one small act of service can burn down mountains of pride.

obstacle two: hungry serpent

Hanuman hadn't flown too far before something that clearly did not belong in the ocean pierced out through surface. It was ghastly, slimy and whopping.

Hanuman stopped abruptly. A demoness lay sprawled in front of him, her mouth wide open. Her intent was to block his way completely with her expansive body. The odor from her mouth was obnoxious enough to kill.

"Glory to the gods! Today they have sent me a big bite. You are my meal for the day. Enter my mouth and satisfy my hunger, *vanara*. Know that I have Lord Brahma's boon that allows me to make a meal of anything that crosses this ocean. You can neither undo the Supreme Creator's blessing nor stop yourself from being my meal. I will savor you, my sweet *vanara* delicacy."[24]

Hanuman had no time to waste arguing with the demoness. He decided to edge past her and carry on with his journey. But she side-stepped and blocked him again. She chortled as she expanded her body by ten times. "My dear *vanara*, you don't have a choice."[25]

Hanuman was in no mood for a conflict. "You must be Surasa, the daughter of Daksha. O great mother of snakes, please understand that I am on a very critical mission. I need to give Mother Sita, whom Ravana has held captive, a message from my Master, Lord

[24] Even when you see someone as a problem, that person may be looking at you as a solution.

[25] The very problems you want to avoid are the ones you must face.

Rama. After delivering the message to Her, I will surrender myself to you and become your meal. Until then, please allow me time. I promise you, I will return to fulfill your desire."[26]

Surasa's hood began to quiver in rage. She flashed her fangs and glared at him with her reddish-brown eyes. Hanuman steadied himself for a not-so-peaceful way of resolving the difference.

Suddenly Hanuman was ten times her size. His sudden resizing clearly shocked Surasa. Her gaping mouth became wider until it was almost twenty times his size. Hanuman then outmatched her by thirty times. She went a notch higher, and her mouth was now forty times as wide. Hanuman outdid her again. The one-upping between the two continued until the wonder-monkey forced her to open her mouth to hundred times its size. Her exceedingly wide mouth and head were now kissing the clouds.[27]

Hanuman realized outdoing her was futile, so he unexpectedly constricted himself to the size of a thumb. He then zoomed into her cavernous tunnel, reached right into her throat and zipped out. The shrinking, the entry and the exit all happened in an eyeblink, which left Surasa with absolutely no reaction time. Hanuman's exit from Surasa's overstretched mouth resembled the luminescent moon exiting the dark mouth of Rahu after the eclipse. Hanuman had depleted not just his size but his ego, too. He quit competing

---

[26] When a leader prioritizes his priorities, success prioritizes him.

[27] According to the magnitude of the problem, one has to readjust the size of one's mind.

The greater the problem, the stronger the mind has to be. Surasa represents the problems we face in life, which tend to get bigger and bigger with time. Hanuman represents the ready mind. Every time the problem grows, the readiness of the mind to face the problem also grows.

with Surasa and realized that it was wiser to take on a humbler approach.[28]

"O daughter of Daksha! O mother of the Nagas! I have fulfilled Brahma's boon without compromising my mission. I have entered your mouth but also exited it. Kindly allow me to proceed on this extremely important mission of finding Sita." With folded hands, Hanuman begged her permission to continue.

Surasa's heart melted. Seeing his humility, she could no longer remain fierce. Surasa spoke to Hanuman calmly. "O gentle *vanara*! Please know that the Devas have sent me to test your valor, caliber, skill, presence of mind, foresight and preparedness for Mission Lanka. Please understand that I have no evil intent. Your demeanor and grace convince me that victory will be yours. I bless that you may succeed in reconnecting Sita with Rama."

Hanuman's face lit up. *Surasa is no enemy; she is an accomplice. She is blessing me as a mother would.*[29]

obstacle three: shadow grabber

Charged with renewed vigor since the Surasa experience, Hanuman rose higher and higher into the sky until he was flying way above anyone was allowed to or was even capable of.

---

[28] One's greatness cannot solve all problems. Some problems are best dealt with humility. The humility software is the best antivirus for the ego bug.

[29] Just a few right words can change one's perception of another person.

The skyways have level-assigned pathways for divine entities. While the Gandharvas fly closest to the earth, the Kinnaras fly a rung higher. The next level is for the *vanaras*; the Siddhas go a level higher. The path higher up is for the Charanas, and even higher for demigods like Ganesh and Kartikeya. The highest of these is for Lord Shiva alone. No one dare fly on Lord Shiva's track. Hanuman was flying along Lord Shiva's path.

The sun shone above him, occasionally casting his shadow on the blue ocean below. Each time a cloud cruised beneath Hanuman, his shadow disappeared from the ocean's surface. The moment Hanuman glided over the cloud, his shadow was on the ocean again. His shadow size appeared larger than even he was.[30]

Hanuman was cruising high over the ocean just fine when suddenly he froze. He was stuck mid-air. No matter how much he tried, he could not move ahead or behind or sideways or downward. He had no idea how; in fact, he was surprised that this even happened.

Then just like that, he was in free fall. The gravitational pull had become intense, almost as if the ocean was dragging him toward itself. The sheer force of it left him with no choice. He let go of all resistance and continued to plunge. He knew that whatever was responsible for his rapid, unhindered drop was deep within the ocean. He was prepared to face anything that came his way now, so he swiveled into dive position to approach the ocean. He pointed his arms above his head, held his hands flat and placed one on top

[30] The kite teaches one that no matter how high one flies, some fine realities will always keep one connected to the ground.

of the other and was all set to hit the waters. The wonder-*vanara* was ready for the excitement ahead.[31]

When he was under a mile away from the surface, a fleshy, gaping mouth sprang out from under the water with a piercing roar. The mouth seemed positioned to swallow the falling hero. Hanuman recognized the creature right away.

Simhika! The dangerous sea monster. The chaya grahi *or shadow grabber! She has managed to grab my shadow and drag me down.* Hanuman remembered Sugriva's warning, and everything made perfect sense to him now. Now all he had to do was follow through with the solution to his problem: to play along with the monster's plan but make slight alterations along the way.[32]

Hanuman accelerated his pace and entered Simhika's mouth much faster than she had anticipated. As he kept going deeper inside her mouth, he kept shrinking. By the time he reached Simhika's gut, Hanuman was very tiny. He could slip in anywhere and everywhere inside her body. So he began moving around rapidly and poking his sharp fingers into all her vital organs. Finally, on reaching her belly, he ripped it open from within and burst out pulling along with him all the innards. Simhika was dead before she realized it.

---

[31] When uncertainty knocks on your door, welcome it with a glass of acceptance rather than hiding inside the closet of fear.

[32] A problem understood is a problem solved.

Just as everybody has a shadow, everybody has a fault. People like Simhika focus on the faults and not on the good qualities in a person. Flying high is indicative of a successful person. Grabbing the shadow is indicative of prioritizing the faults of a successful person. Pulling down a high-flying individual is indicative of defaming the person.

Exploding out of the water, Hanuman continued his sojourn toward Lanka. Something sinister was awaiting him… something that none could see, but which could see everything…

LESSONS FROM HANUMAN'S JUMP

We can view Hanuman's jump across the ocean from two main perspectives, and each offers valuable lessons.

Life Perspective

Everyone has some mission to accomplish in life. No matter how small or big the mission, obstacles will come along the way, making it a challenge to complete. Each mission has the same obstacles as the ones Hanuman faced.

Obstacle One: Everyone *lacks confidence* before executing a seemingly impossible mission. To overcome this, we need a Jambavan-like mentor to reassure us of our powers and remind us of past victories.

Obstacle Two: There is considerable *distance between where we are and where we want to be.* The gap seems so huge that it becomes difficult to decide on when and how to take the first step. To overcome this, we need to take a leap of faith. Before taking this leap of faith, Hanuman readied himself by praying. Praying is an act of mental preparation, which empowers us to take that leap.

Obstacle Three: From time to time, everyone faces a *mental block.* It's called the golden-mountain block. Anyone intensely pursuing a mission encounters this golden mountain. This block slows us down during the mission as a warning that rushing at a frantic pace could burn us out. This golden mountain actually represents the mental inertia that tries to slow us down. It sometimes comes in the form of a breakdown, sometimes as a desire for comfort, sometimes as distractions and temptations. The only way to deal with this block is through single-minded focus on the goal. No temptation is worth losing the goal. For Hanuman, his mission was more important than his comfort. That obsession to reach our destination melts all blocks away.

Obstacle Four: Just when we are about to reach our goal, we experience a *competitive mentality*. People like Surasa love to instigate this mentality so that we lose sight of our goal and find ourselves stuck in needless competition. A competitive mentality forces us to think that victory is about proving and establishing that we are better than everyone around. The mentality becomes so fierce at times that we allow it to consume us at the cost of our goal. Hanuman dealt with competitive mentality by letting go. When we let go of the desire to prove our superiority, our mind automatically becomes tranquil and refocuses on the goal. By letting go of the petty desire to prove our superiority, we can embrace the superior desire to prioritize our mission.

Obstacle Five: Something that can often obstruct our mission path is *envy*. Envy begins with faultfinding and ends in cruelty. When we achieve any kind of success, we tend to become envious of anyone ahead of us. Flying high indicates achieving heights of success. Hanuman is flying high and Simhika is way below. The shadow represents our faults. No matter how highly successful we are, there will always be some fault or weakness. Instead of looking up and admiring the success of the person, people like Simhika prefer to look down on the faults of that person. Catching hold of the shadow represents criticism. Pulling down the person indicates defaming a person by criticizing him or her. Envy prevents us from being inspired by successful people. Hanuman did not allow envy to emerge. He checked it immediately. He made Simhika become humble. Rather than envying those who are successful, we should learn to celebrate their successes. Celebrating others' successes soon leads to celebrating our own successes. Plotting for another's failure indicates our own failure.

Spiritual Perspective

Hanuman's leap and the obstacles that he came across when seen from a spiritual point of view represent the challenges a spiritual aspirant (*sadhaka*) goes through before reaching his or her final destination.

Spiritually, the goal to be achieved is Sita, who represents *bhaktidevi* or the goddess of devotion. Unlike the life perspective, the obstacles here are all internal. These obstacles represent the inner struggles of a *sadhaka* while on the path of devotion.

Challenge One: When it comes to matters of spirituality, everyone *struggles with self-doubt*. At such a time, words of inspiration can work wonders. The words of inspiration of a mentor or *shiksha guru* serve as the impetus through our long journey of spirituality. Jambavan reminded Hanuman not only of his powers but also about why the gods first granted and later denied him those powers. The gods blessed Hanuman with unlimited powers when he was small, but a sage's curse erased all memories of those powers. Hanuman had been abusing his powers for his entertainment. The sage cursed him that he would not remember anything about any of his powers until someone came into his life to channelize his powers for a mission. Jambavan is a guru who channelizes a *sadhaka*'s power to the service of the Lord.

Challenge Two: The vast ocean represents *deha abhiman* or *pride in one's own greatness*, which is a big barrier to being completely devoted to God. All the great *vanaras* expressed their inability to cross the ocean, indicating that even the most powerful people have great difficulty in overcoming this big impediment. Hanuman considered himself an arrow. An arrow by itself cannot achieve much and cannot travel a long distance. The distance an arrow travels depends entirely on the skill and arm strength of the shooter. When he jumped across the ocean, Hanuman felt like Lord Rama's arrow. According to him, it wasn't his ability that enabled him to cross over the ocean, but it was Rama's power that helped him do so. He chanted "Rama!" He started with "Ra," and he ended with "ma." When he reached "ma," he was already in Lanka. To accomplish what even great people couldn't, Hanuman had to have *dhairyam* or courage. As *sadhakas*, we should develop the courage to want to get out of the bodily concept of life that binds us in the shackles of our own greatness.

Challenge Three: One of the things that obstruct one's vision of the goal is *the lure of glitter*. While practicing spiritual discipline, we are bound to come across some fringe benefits – adoration, worship, comfort and pleasures. Pleasure by itself is not bad, but when it takes us away from our spiritual pursuits, we must avoid it. We begin to take these fringe benefits seriously and lose focus on our goals. Good things are not always good. When good comes in the way of executing our duty, then it becomes bad. A *sadhaka* should develop *drishtih* or far-sightedness. Although the golden mountain offered to him a glittering proposal, Hanuman kept his vision focused on his goal of devotion and avoided all the fringe benefits.

Challenge Four: During our spiritual journey, we often find it difficult to *control our pride and stay humble*. Hanuman's interaction with Surasa teaches a *sadhaka* these very insightful lessons. The first is that Surasa and Hanuman competed with each other to prove that one was bigger than the other. Becoming big represents the act of helping others. Two do-gooders tend to compete with one another to prove their superiority in doing good. Although doing good is important, good that makes you proud is not actually good. When Hanuman realized the futility of one-upmanship, he made himself very small, thereby shrinking his pride of being a doer. When doing good for others, we should become extremely humble and small. Rather than being arrogant about doing good, we should cultivate humility, for we are merely instruments and not the cause.

Challenge Five: For a *sadhaka*, it is a challenge *to remain detached as well as use intelligence*. Surasa told Hanuman that he was a detached *sadhaka* and he ought not bother about his body and allow her to eat him. Hanuman, however, responded by saying that he would offer his body as her meal but only after accomplishing his mission of meeting Sita, conveying Rama's message to Her and Her message to Rama. He admitted that a *sadhaka* was neither afraid of death nor attached to the body, but an intelligent *sadhaka* knows better than to underestimate the worth of the body. A wise *sadhaka* would fearlessly give up the body only after it has served its purpose and accomplished its goal. Our body is like a boat that helps us cross the river of material existence. After we cross the river, the boat becomes useless and we should detach from it. A *sadhaka* should develop *matih* or *resourceful intelligence*. Although Surasa challenged him in many ways, Hanuman used his intelligence to overcome all the obstacles she posed and technically satisfied all her demands without compromising on his principles and goals.

We are never envious of another's spiritual qualities, but rather of another's material qualities. At the spiritual level, envy can never exist because we understand that every good quality is simply a spark of God's splendor. Simhika caught Hanuman's shadow, which represents a fault. She managed to find a fault where none existed. While the demigods had sent Surasa to test Hanuman, Simhika was sent by the demons to obstruct him. Simhika was the mother of Rahu. Just as her son Rahu was envious of the demigods' success in retrieving all the nectar from the churning of the milk ocean, Simhika was envious of Hanuman's success in flying across the ocean. Just as Rahu disguised himself and tried to cheat Mohini Murti, Simhika hid herself inside the ocean and tried to cheat Hanuman. While he dealt with Surasa using *matih*, he dealt with Simhika using *dakshyam* or expertise. He executed her without her realizing it. Envy is a demoniac obstacle. It must be eliminated to progress spiritually.

Just as Hanuman used his intelligence to deal with various obstacles along his way, a *sadhaka* must use intelligence to counter subtle obstacles that come in the path of devotion. In overcoming each subtle obstacle, a *sadhaka* comes closer to the goal of life: loving devotion to the Lord.

Chapter 2

Freedom and Futility in the Golden Kingdom

blessings from death and justice

He landed with a soft thud! But…

WHAAAAAAM!

Before he could even regain his balance or catch his breath, the hard kick on his back toppled him. His warrior instincts took over instantly, and he leaped. A warrior's life was without rest. He had only just completed a long and arduous journey, and here he was facing a new challenge. One moment he was on the ground, the next he was up on his feet. He stood with his arms in combat position, ready for a duel with the invisible enemy. In front of him was thick mist and nothing else. Whoever, or whatever, threw that kick was hiding right behind it.

Suddenly something gross and fearsome stepped out of the mist. Hanuman relaxed. "O Mrityudev! O god of death! I can't believe it's you! Why would you be on Ravana's island? And why would you kick me?"

The ice-cold stare gave way to a compassionate look of recognition. "O son of Vayu! O *Pavanaputra*! What have I done? Please forgive me for inadvertently kicking a gentle soul such as you. I know that you have my boon that prevents death from touching you. But what do I do? I am Ravana's prisoner. I am so helpless. I no longer have the freedom to do what I want. Ravana has enchained me to this mountain with Rudra *mantras* and has instructed me to kill anyone who dares step in here. No matter how much I try, I am unable to break free from these shackles."[1]

One touch by Hanuman and the Rudra *mantra* shackles fell off. Yama was free again. Ravana's foresight and strategy impressed Hanuman. Yama was so grateful to his savior that he blessed him with fearlessness. "Anyone who remembers you will never be afraid of death. I will protect whoever follows you." Saying this, Yama disappeared in a blink. He did not want Ravana to trap him again.

The mountain twins, Lamba and Suvela, formed the northern borders of Lanka. They were the first walls of the forbidden island. Stationing Yama there was strategic. Who could possibly escape the gaze of death? With Yama having escaped, the entry point was barrier free. Ravana of course would know of this only after it was too late. Yama's departure had freed Suvela from the atrocities of the god of death but made Ravana susceptible to death itself.[2]

---

[1] Those who become prisoners of others' desires butcher their own conscience.

[2] Security breaches do not happen when walls are broken down but when guards are broken.

While ordinary people busy themselves with preventing intruders from entering their houses, intelligent people focus on preventing corrupt intrusion into their minds.

Just as Hanuman was about to move into the city of Lanka, he heard something. He stood still! *There, I can hear it again*! The voice was feeble, but Hanuman's keen ears had picked it up. As he stepped toward that direction, the voice became clearer and louder. It seemed to come from a cave on the mountain. He ran toward it not knowing what to expect, but he could sense desperation in that imploring voice.

Hanging upside down from the roof of the cave was someone with his face closely staring at the wall. His intricately enchained hands and legs ensured he was immobile.

"Please help me!"

Yet another of Ravana's prisoners! Hanuman unhooked the chains off the ceiling and carefully lay the suffering being down. Hanuman then turned him around to catch a glimpse of his face. It was Shani, the god of justice – the one whose infamous stare reduces people to nothing was now reduced to nothing. Everything seemed so clear to Hanuman.

Ravana, who was also an astrology scholar, knew the power of Shani's stare. He knew that the god of justice glanced favorably at an individual for two-and-a-half years and unfavorably for the next two-and-a-half years. Ravana timed his visit to Shani's abode to match the phase when the god's glance was favorable toward him. He then imprisoned and bound Shani to save himself from the adverse glances of the harbinger of misfortune forever. He did not want Shani to cast his bad eye on him or anyone or anything in Lanka. Ravana tied him up and hung him upside down in a way that his gaze remained fixed on the wall of the cave on the edge of his kingdom.[3]

Shani's profuse expression of gratitude toward his rescuer Hanuman reflected huge relief after months of torture. "Anyone who remembers you will never be affected by the miseries caused by my glance." The god of justice blessed his savior. Shani was free to escape, but he chose to stay on in the mountain for a while. "Once you accomplish your mission on this island, help me by selecting an area in Lanka to cast my harmful gaze. Ravana will suffer for trying to manipulate it," he requested Hanuman.[4]

With two immediate problems solved and two invaluable blessings gained, Hanuman turned his focus to the main task. He looked ahead toward the center of the island. He had conquered three mountain peaks in the last few days, and the fourth was right in front of him. From the summit he was on, he could see the dazzling golden city of Lanka, which loomed from the heights of the Trikuta mountain. The Trikuta peak was so high that it almost felt as if Lanka was resting on the clouds. Hanuman could not but be fascinated by this architectural wonder. Vishwakarma had outclassed himself, having created this city with not only his hands but also his highly ingenious mind. Lanka was a million times superior to Amravati, the abode of Indra.

---

[3] Those who think luck brings them success do not know whom to blame for their failures.

[4] Instead of working hard on manipulating the luck factor, one should be working hard.

Shani represents the luck factor. Ravana tried to control the luck factor by controlling Shani's glance.

Three Peaks and One

Hanuman scaled three peaks during his journey to Lanka. He had conquered the first peak along with the *vanaras* when they were lost and thirsty. They had found Swayamprabha's cave. The second was the Mahendra mountain, the one from which he had taken his giant leap across the ocean. He had most recently scaled the third or twin peaks of Subela and Lamba to survey Lanka.

Each of the peaks is symbolic of a virtue. While the first peak signifies *faith*, the second symbolizes *thought* and the third represents *renunciation*. To reach Sita, who represents *bhakti*, a devotee has to climb these three peaks first.

One must scale these three peaks at important junctures in life. One must conquer the peak of faith when surrounded by doubt. The forest represents doubt. The *vanaras* were lost in the forest of doubt and had no idea if they were ever going to make it alive, let alone finding Sita. It was during this crisis that Hanuman taught them to climb the peak of faith. On the peak of faith, they found a cave that represented *mercy*. Only when you ascend the peak of faith can mercy descend into your life.

Attachment to the body is like a massive ocean that is difficult to cross. To be able to jump across such a massive ocean of attachments, one needs to climb the mountain of high thoughts. Only from a higher plane of thought can one jump across the ocean of bodily attachments. Most people are so attached to the body and mind that they remain stuck in the depths of the ocean of attachments. Only when one crosses over the ocean of bodily attachments can *bhakti* be attained.

To ordinary people, Lanka appears to be an indestructible place, but when Hanuman spotted Lanka from atop the peak of renunciation, he realized that it was destructible. Those who see God as the only eternal object and everything in this world as destructible, the temporary objects of this world cannot lure them. Only when one sees the world through the eyes of renunciation can one avoid being enamored by the glitter of this world and lose sight of Sita or *bhakti*.

To attain *bhakti* or devotion, one must first climb the peak of faith where mercy is available. From there one gains access to higher thoughts that help cross the ocean of attachments. Finally, those high thoughts help develop the will to renounce the attraction of worldly objects and focus on devotion to the Lord.

The fourth peak is the one on which Ravana is seated. The Trikuta mountain represents false ego. Because Ravana was atop the peak of false ego, he wasn't able to recognize *bhakti* even though she was in Lanka. *Bhakti* becomes inaccessible to those steeped in ego.

all that glitters...

Between the twin peaks he was on and the one he wanted to reach, lay a vast forest. Reaching Ravana was never going to be easy. Hanuman realized that unlike normal kings who build huge forts, Ravana utilized the ocean and the forest as natural barriers. Any enemy would first have to cross *jala durga*[5] and then the *vana durga*.[6] When Hanuman surveyed the vast forest in front of him,

[5] The watery fortress.

[6] The forest fortress.

he could see the extent to which Ravana had manipulated nature. Generally, flowers and fruits are seasonal, but in Lanka, every tree bore fruits and flowers off season for fear of Ravana.[7]

High above the green forest carpet stood the proud city of Lanka with its massive shimmering palaces and tall shiny buildings. Every palace had a golden dome. Hanuman thought these palaces were bedazzling. *Each of these huge palaces looks like a temple of serious worship.* He realized that the *rakshasas* residing in these palaces were worshippers of *sharira devata* or the body itself.[8]

As Hanuman stood staring at the palaces in Lanka from the mountain peak he was perched on, he tried to fathom the wonder and splendor spread out in front of him. *This place is so fascinating. It appears even better than Ayodhya! Such an opulent place should belong to Rama. The city of Lanka appears like a beautiful bedecked woman. I can't ever remember having any material desires, but this city seems to be evoking some shockingly serious stay-back vibes in me. It's home to demons, but its prosperity and opulence make it seem like a* punya bhumi.[9] *In comparison to the enthralling Lanka, my home, the kingdom of Kishkinda, is made of sticks and stones. Between the ocean and the super secure Lanka, where will I find Sita? When Ravana has managed to capture and torture even the demigods who can't imagine conquering Lanka, how can a group of untrained* vanaras *find Sita? Even if Rama Himself came here, what would He be able to accomplish?*

---

[7] Man tries to outwit the simplicity of nature with the complexity of his mind.

[8] The acharyas explain that just as the body, no matter how good it looks, has to be burned at the time of death, the temple where the body is worshipped, no matter how opulent, has to be burned ultimately.

[9] Pious place.

With each passing moment, and the longer he stared out at the lush golden city, the negative buzz inside Hanuman's mind began to grow louder. *The city has such tight security because of the limitless ocean and the sea of demons. I can think of only four among the million* vanara *soldiers who are even capable of reaching it. What can Angad, Sugriva, Nila and I accomplish in this demon's impenetrable fortress?*

Four Ways to Conquer the Enemy

Saama, *daana*, *danda* and *bheda* are the four ways of winning over the enemy. But these are pointless against the demons of Lanka. For *Saama* or compromise to have any effect, the enemy needs to have some *sattva guna* or the virtue of goodness. Any discussion can be fruitful only when passion and ignorance are kept aside, but these demons are soaked in passion and ignorance, which can never help reach an alliance or peace.

Daana or charity is for someone weaker or in need of something. These demons are never in any need, and they "grab" what they want. Of what use is *daana* to someone with much greater strength?

Danda or punishment is futile against *rakshasa*s who are ace magicians, who never fight fair, and who always use treachery and trickery.

Bheda or dissent is unlikely to work on them either. To create in-fights between the demons, they need to disagree. The unfortunate reality is that good people always seem to differ with each other whereas bad people are terribly united. Dividing people with such unity is impossible. There are multiple ways for doing good, but limited ways for doing bad. Is that why good people never seem to agree on how to do good and bad people unanimously agree on the plan to do bad? If *saama*, *daana*, *danda* and *bheda* are not possible, then nothing is!

of shapes and sizes

As a tornado of negative thoughts began swirling inside his head, Hanuman began to feel exhausted with confusion. He calmed himself down with some self-talk. *Why am I becoming so negative right at the onset? I haven't even entered Lanka and don't even know if Sita is alive. I need to first find Her, and if She is alive, I can proceed with a plan from thereon. But right now, I need to find a way to break into the impenetrable golden city.*[10]

It makes no sense to enter the city in daylight. I need to wait until nightfall. The night exposes everyone's shortcomings. I need all the patience I can muster. Haste will put to waste the months and months of effort by Lord Rama and the millions of vanaras."

Hanuman turned toward the sun. It had begun to set. He realized he had to strategize really quickly now. *I must assume a form that will arouse the least suspicion for me to remain undetected by the demons. The only way I can do that is by fooling them. It's acceptable to trick tricksters. Should I take on the form of Ravana himself? No, that's too risky. Too many people will come to meet me as I walk around. How about I become a* rakshasa? *I could go undetected. No, even that is risky. The* rakshasa gandha[11] *is distinct. I can assume their form but not their smell. Going in as a* vanara *is also dangerous, as it will reveal my intention and my identity right away. I need to go undetected till I find Sita. I need to become something very tiny and not arouse suspicion.*

---

[10] A highly negative mind is a like a baby. You never know when it will spray you with the urine of foul thoughts.

[11] Demon odor.

Flexibility Is Key

When Hanuman grew to acquire gigantic proportions, Simhika grabbed him, and when he shrunk and became tiny, Lankini caught him. He realized that walking into Lanka was dangerous.

If big, people want to trip you, and if tiny, people want to eat you up. This is exactly what happens in the world. Everyone is out to bring down a great person and crush and consume a humble person.

The question then is how to behave in a world where people will create obstacles no matter what. Should one be big or small? Hanuman shows us the way by being flexible. He can be both big and small. His attachment is not to his form but to his goal. He is ready to take any form that helps him achieve that. Such flexibility is the key. One must keep on going toward one's goal and not be perturbed by people's reactions and treatment.

Hanuman suddenly stood up! As the sun kept sinking into the ocean, Hanuman kept shrinking. The moment the sun submerged completely, in place of the mighty hero stood a small cat-sized *vanara*. The tiny creature wasted no time and scurried down to the mountain toward the golden city. Hanuman could feel this intense thrill build up inside from the excitement of having found the right disguise and the fear of being discovered. He was now ready for what lay ahead and looked forward to the great adventures in this dangerous land of the demons. As he stealthily leaped and skipped through the forest toward the gates of Lanka, the moon gave him company by chasing after him and lighting up his path.[12]

[12] Any venture becomes a thrilling adventure when the fear of failure exceeds the chances of success. Fear induces excitement as well as determination.

not on her watch

The gates were within reach now. *Nobody is likely to spot a tiny monkey, let alone give a second glance.* Smug about his assumption, Hanuman walked confidently toward the gates. Just as he was about to place one foot into the opening between the bars of the gate, a metal slammed heavily in front of him. He moved backward with a jolt. A heavy trident shaft pierced the ground, missing his extended foot by a whisker. The throw was so intense and powerful that the rest of the iron shaft continued to vibrate vigorously even after the pointy end had penetrated the ground. Two large blood-shot eyes were staring down at Hanuman in burning rage.[13]

"I am Lankini, the guardian of Lanka. Nothing and no one can enter the city without my sanction and Ravana's will. Who are you? Why are you trying to trespass?" Lankini's hoarse voice and ghastly appearance brought a dreadful eeriness to the beautiful moonlit night. Lankini was as horrendous as Lanka was wonderful.

On realizing the only way of entering the city was not by confronting her, Hanuman feigned innocence. "I am a *vanara* as you can see. I have always lived in the forests and mountains and have never seen a city. I hear that Lanka is mesmerizing. I am very curious to see a city. Please allow me to spend some time in the city before I leave. I promise not to disturb anyone inside. I will look around, eat a few fruits and return to the forest. I have heard that Lanka is home to some of the best succulent mangoes."[14]

---

[13] When a hero walks into trouble, he takes it as grace.
When a fool steps into grace, he takes it as trouble.

[14] Curiosity may kill the cat, but fear paralyses the mouse. It is better to die than live a life stunned by ignorance.

Lankini guffawed at the *vanara*'s request. "If all you want is fruits, then I will get you as many as you want right here, outside this gate. No one steps in without the will of Ravana. Not even you, monkey."

She was adamant, so Hanuman changed his tone. He knew that *rakshasas* did not understand requests and would better respond to threats. "If you allow me to go in peacefully, I promise you that I will not create any disturbance inside. If you do not, I will force my way in. I am a *vanara*, and once I decide to do something no one can stop me."[15]

Both the change of tone and the threat were not lost on Lankini. Enraged, she rushed toward the little *vanara* and shoved him away from the gate with great force. Her speed caught him off guard, and he found his tiny frame hurled a great distance away. As he slid across the mud, Hanuman regained his balance. Now he was in battle mode. He clenched his fist, ran toward the towering demoness, leaped up into the air and landed a hard punch across her jaw with his left fist. As he landed back in position, from the corner of his eyes he caught a glimpse of Lankini's gigantic body plopping to the ground. He had knocked her out with a single punch.[16]

A minute later, a dazed and wrecked Lankini grasped the very gate that she dearly guarded and pulled herself up. Standing in front

---

[15] Humans speak the language of request, whereas animals speak the language of threat.

But animalistic humans speak the language of threat, and humanistic animals speak the language of kindness.

[16] Sometimes sense cannot be taught to people but needs to be punched into them.

of Hanuman was a humble demoness with folded palms, begging for mercy. Her eyes seemed to say, "Please don't hit me anymore." Hanuman relaxed as he unclenched his fists and facial muscles. He knew a discussion was now possible. Her lofty ego was no longer a barrier to any conversation.[17]

"I had been waiting for this day since forever! I knew this would happen." Lankini's post-attack statement baffled Hanuman. *What does she even mean? What is she referring to?* Lankini was on a confession spree, and there was no stopping her. "Even in my previous life, I was a guard at a gate. Not the gates of Lanka but of Lord Brahma's abode. While there, I had become arrogant and haughty. I was so consumed by the power of my position that I began to mistreat everyone. Lord Brahma, my master, was quite angered by my attitude as he knew that it went against the intrinsic humility of *Brahmaloka* and embraced the brashness of *rakshasaloka*. So, he wasted no time and banished me to life as a gatekeeper in Lanka. He justified his decision by saying that my ego would be purified over time by coexisting with those with larger egos than mine.[18]

I realized my folly and begged forgiveness. I implored him for a concession. The curse could not be undone, but then he pacified me saying that I would be liberated from the curse the day a *vanara* would arrive in Lanka and punch me. He also told me that the day would mark the beginning of the end of the kingdom of Lanka. Thank you, o *vanara*, for freeing me. I bless you and wish you success in all your ventures in Lanka. The *rakshasa*s are dead. From the day

---

[17] Discussion is not possible when the scream of ego is too loud.

[18] High-class clothes don't necessarily mean high-class mindsets.

Ravana brought Sita here, I have known that She would be the cause of Lanka's fall."[19]

Hanuman smiled. Lankini's words were proof that Sita was in Lanka. Sampati was after all an old vulture and not much faith could be placed on his vision. But now that Lankini had reconfirmed it, there was great hope. Hanuman could now explore the city all he wanted and find Mother Sita. Lankini disappeared instantly, leaving Hanuman alone in the company of the moon once again.

Lessons from the Lankini Encounter

A single moment of association with Hanuman transformed Lankini much more than wisdom from countless books ever could. Great people deliver deep and life-changing messages with subtlety.

Satsang, or association with great people, transforms us in four different ways.

1. The primary purpose of *satsang* is to challenge the belief systems entrenched within our intellect. Many of these deeply embedded beliefs are those that we follow without logicizing or questioning. We accept these as absolute truths. Lankini believed her loyalty lay with her master Ravana, who fed her. She sincerely performed her job of guarding Lanka keeping this belief in mind. When Hanuman punched her, he made her realize that her devotion to the master (*swami bhakti*) was good, but it was first important to ascertain who was a worthy master. She was following the principles of *dharma* without really understanding its spirit. Lankini believed that she was

[19] Our actions are either digging a grave or building a skyscraper.

following the path of *dharma* by loyally serving her master when, in fact, she was merely justifying her belief that Ravana was her master and she was his servant. A good servant is one who can identify a worthy master. Until she met Hanuman, she believed Ravana was the master and anyone entering Lanka without his permission was a trespasser. But after her encounter with Hanuman, she realized that Ravana was the real trespasser.

2. The second purpose is to reduce our attachments. Lankini was attached to Lanka and her role as the protector of Lanka. A moment's association with Hanuman made her detach herself from her position and her attachment to the land that she worshipped.

3. The third is to help one rise from a fall. Satsang does not allow you to remain fallen, but it encourages you to rise to a higher platform. Lankini fell when Hanuman punched her, but she also found the strength to stand up and thank him for bringing her to her senses by hitting her. Usually, no one considers being hit or humiliated as fortunate. Most find honor fortunate and dishonor unfortunate. But a misfortune that helps you remember God is a fortune, and a fortune that makes you forget God is a misfortune.

4. Satsang removes the deep effect of negative association. Lankini was not bad, but her association with Ravana made her bad. Hanuman's involvement undid that Ravana-linked damage to her consciousness and helped recollect her memories. She instantly remembered her past life in Lord Brahma's company. Our relationship with God is not new, but we forget that bond. We need a saint like Hanuman to remind us of that link with God.

The presiding deity of Lanka, Lankini, represents egotism. Just as she guards Lanka under Ravana's command, egotism is under the control of the mind. Just as she prevents the entry of Hanuman into Lanka, egotism prevents the entry of a guru into our lives. Initially, Hanuman tries to gently talk her into letting him inside, but when she displays her arrogance, his approach becomes tough. Similarly, the guru tries to transform our lives gently. But when we exhibit arrogance and aversion toward him, he weighs on our ego. When the ego is subjugated, whims of the mind will soon perish.

hiding to seek

An unguarded gate and a heavily guarded city awaited Hanuman. So he decided not to enter through the city gate and scaled the wall instead. Leaping onto the high wall of the city, Hanuman jumped in. Wanting to bring as much inauspiciousness into the golden city as he possibly could, he purposely landed with his left foot first.[20]

No sooner than he stepped into the city, music began to fill his ears. The city was alive! The older the night became, the younger the city seemed to appear. The intensity of the nightlife in Lanka was insane. Sounds of intoxicated laughter and loud music merged and

[20] According to the *shastras*, one should start anything, such as going on a travel, wedding and *griha-pravesha*, by setting the right foot first, but when entering into the abode of an enemy, one should put the left foot forward and enter through an opening other than the main entrance to ensure victory.

emanated from every nook of the city. Mist hung over the houses, giving Lanka a celestial look. The gold and diamonds embedded into rooftops and walls enhanced the opulence. Every building – from small huts to massive palaces – was unique. Hanuman could hear the beats of music and the tinkling of women's jewelry in every house that he passed by. Occasionally, he could hear the claps and roars of the *rakshasa* men moving to rhythm.

Much of the city was immersed in revelries, but a section was into some serious secret business. Hanuman saw clusters of *rakshasa* men in different places chant serious mantras and Vedic rituals for the prosperity of the king and his city. While some men had matted hair, others had shaved heads, and they all wore clothes made of cowhide. All of them also held some instrument used for worship. While some held *kusa* grass in their hands, others held fire vessels used for sacrifices. The king's armed men guarded these secret rituals. Ravana enforced such rituals to retain the prosperity of his kingdom.[21]

Lanka's leaders lived in palaces that were a million times more opulent and were built in exclusive areas far away from the common hubbub. As an innocent and curious little monkey roaming the streets of Lanka, Hanuman entered the palaces and conducted thorough searches, he made a mental note of everything – the security measures, the number of guards, various entry and exit points and such. Ravana's spies, though experts, failed to notice the tiny *vanara* who was conducting a stealth recce of Lanka, even as they minutely surveyed and combed every millimeter of Lanka.[22]

---

[21] More important than attaining prosperity is retaining prosperity. Prosperity is attained by talent and retained by character.

[22] While looking for big problems, one overlooks small threats.

As he continued his exploration and analysis, evading the prying eyes of the surveillance teams, Hanuman spotted a massive cylindrical structure that seemed quite different from the usual palaces in the city. So, he scrambled up to its terrace for a better assessment. He knew he had to expect the unexpected, but he still wasn't prepared for what he was witnessing. Though not encouraging, he knew the view had given him an inside edge unlike any he had imagined possible in this mission. Colluding below was a monstrous gathering of the most rugged of all *rakshasa*s he had ever seen. Hanuman knew right away that he was staring down at, and being privy to, a secret drill of the most confidential division of the Lankan army. The opponent was much more formidable than he had expected. So, he quickly began to carefully assess the demons in the various divisions. This was going to be no easy army to defeat, and the mere thought of a bunch of *vanara*s facing this barbaric army was extremely unsettling.

As Hanuman observed the *rakshasa*s of various sizes, shapes and demeanors, he noticed that those with similar attributes were clubbed together to form battalions. So, the stern ones, the creepy ones, the scary ones, the ghastly ones and the ones with hideous deformities and unkempt and wild hairstyles formed different divisions. There were divisions of those with one eye and one ear. There was even one comprising those with only an eye and an ear. One troop comprised *rakshasa* midgets with bows and arrows. Hanuman understood this was a ploy to use their short stature as an advantage against the enemies, considering these *rakshasa*s could work as snipers – shoot from concealed positions without being seen. Besides the troop comprising these physically challenged marksmen were teams categorized according to the weapons the *rakshasa*s wielded. So there were troops each for those with swords, clubs, pestles, hammers, javelins, tree weapons, thunderbolts, hand slings, nooses and spikes. One look, and Hanuman knew that these demons were all highly adept at using the weapons they carried. [23]

As he stood on the terrace wall of that army safe house, the corner of his eye caught a glimmer at a distance. He turned around to see the most dazzling structure he had ever come across. He reasoned that effulgent section was probably the center of the kingdom of Lanka, the capital city of the land. He had guessed right. It was the personal bastion of the king of Lanka, Ravana. This sparkly portion was so much more magnificent and luxurious than the rest of Lanka. Every other opulent palace Hanuman had seen thus far seemed utterly worthless. He noticed that while the rest of Lanka's settlements were along the base of the Trikuta Mountain, Ravana's palace was on the summit. He also noticed that the city's grandeur increased along the height of the mountain and peaked at the pinnacle – the grandest section of all. The planning of the city astounded even the well-travelled Hanuman.

Although everything was admiration-worthy, Hanuman knew he was here on a job. He leaped off the secret terrace and began to race toward the glimmering central city, realizing that he had wasted too much time searching for Sita everywhere else. It was so clear to him now that Ravana would have kept Her somewhere within inner city limits, somewhere not far from himself. Moreover, that would have to be the most secure part of Lanka and the most fiercely protected.

On reaching the restricted territory, Hanuman noticed that much of the sparkling royal enclave was occupied by Ravana's golden palace, which had simpler buildings that housed support staff and

---

[23] A good team is organized chaos. Everyone looks chaotically different but is organized in his or her vision.

administrators around it. A large moat with floating white lotuses and blood-thirsty aquatic creatures surrounded the palace.[24]

The golden palace had amazing archways plated with rare metals and embedded with precious stones. Each entrance was unique and different. Chariots, elephants and palanquins lined the entrances and were at the ready for the king's orders. Protective shields covered with lion and tiger skin and crossed elephant tusks adorned the walls. Alert palace guards marched along the hallways, constantly on the lookout for suspicious movement. Security chariots surveyed the palace compound with tremulous movements that would scare even the smartest of intruders.

The palace gardens were filled with rare species of birds and animals, the kind Hanuman had never seen. He wondered if these creatures even belonged to the universe he knew. The female aides who went in and out of the palace and out in the courtyard, carrying out various chores were the flawlessly beautiful. The tinkles and jingles from their gold trinkets and anklets seemed to create a kind music that made the atmosphere sensuous. The mesmerizing fragrance from the perfume on these women and the flowers in the palace gardens permeated the environment. Musical instruments played in perfect unison in the background from all around the outer wall of the palace, which caused hearts to beat to the rhythm. From within Ravana's palace, came sounds that resembled those emanating from the mysterious depths of the ocean.

Not wanting to enter the palace without studying the security protocols, Hanuman stealthily walked around the palace building,

---

[24] The most beautiful things conceal the most dangerous realities. Around every beauty lies something ugly, and around every danger lies hope.

scrutinizing every inch of it. He noticed square buildings at regular intervals, which housed various types of lethal weapons that could be easily accessed by the security personnel during emergencies. He also noticed that the construction of the palace followed all the norms of *shilpa shastra*,[25] which ensured flawlessness, perfection, security and sheer artistry. Ravana's golden palace seemed like a slice of heaven on earth. It shone so beautifully that no one bothered to glance at the moon as it appeared pale in comparison.[26]

As Hanuman turned around a corner, something dazzling caught his eye. It was astoundingly beautiful and seemed like a huge chandelier suspended in air. The contraption, with a body of pure gold, pillars of silver, a canopy made of precious stones and seats made of the *vaidurya* stone, was a sight to behold. Hanuman knew right away that it was the famed *pushpak vimana*, and that Ravana was proudly flaunting it outside his palace for everyone to see, admire and envy![27]

The celestial architect Vishwakarma, the maker of the flying machine, was so impressed with his own creation that he called it a masterpiece. Nothing about this machine was easy. Each minute part required extreme effort and intelligence to create. The flying machine resembled a swan. Numerous smaller silver- and coral-carved birds with precious stones in their beaks were placed along the sides of the carrier. The wings were designed to give off a playful vibe. On either side of the flying machine were carvings of two huge silver elephants offering a lotus flower made of precious stones to

---

[25] A scripture pertaining to architecture and artistry.

[26] We are so busy looking at luminaries that we fail to see ordinary people with luminous qualities.

[27] Possessions that make you happy when you see pain in others' eyes are brand ambassadors of envy.

an image of Lakshmi, which was right at the center of the plane.

Hanuman chuckled at the image of Lakshmi. *How foolish of this man to have abducted the real Lakshmi yet worship Her image!* Hanuman remembered soon enough that the plane didn't really belong to Ravana and that he had stolen it from his stepbrother Kubera, an ardent worshipper of Lakshmi.[28]

The flying machine was parked right outside the palace building terrace. A small ramp on the edge of the terrace led right into the flying chariot. Ravana could just walk into his prized possession. Despite Ravana's demoniac mindset and evil intentions, Hanuman could not help but appreciate the demon king's refined tastes and brilliant brain. Ravana had built for himself a unique and the only flying chariot on earth with technology so advanced that it could be controlled by the thoughts of its owner. Thought sensors accurately identified where the owner wanted to go and flew to the desired destination. The flying chariot also customized its size to suit the number of passengers. It seemed like a carrier in which no one wanted to reach any destination, in which sages could meditate until forever.[29]

Hanuman hadn't even realized that his inspection had led him right inside the flying chariot. There he was in the very *pushpak vimana* in which Ravana had brought Sita from Panchavati to Lanka. Suddenly it hit him that Sita was still to be found. He jumped off the magnificent suspended chariot that had perhaps sucked him in like a magnet and hopped onto the terrace. As he tried to find a

---

[28] When you try to steal prosperity from others, peace is stolen from you.

[29] Rather than wanting machines that sense your thoughts, one should aspire for machines that put sense into one's thoughts.

way out, he understood that Ravana had a few more celestial cars and chariots, all suspended along the terrace of his palace.

Thus far, Hanuman had managed to lay low and deftly dodge curious eyes, taking great care not to raise any suspicion at all. Now that he was in the lion's den – the very core of Ravana's abode – he knew he had to double up on the covertness. It was no small plot of land. Rather, it was massive, with a width of half a *yojana* and a length of a full *yojana*. *Even Brahma and Indra probably don't have a palace this big*. Hanuman wondered as he wandered.

As soon as Hanuman made his way down from the terrace into the palace building, a whiff of cool air hit him. He could feel the drastic change in temperature, and one look at the *chandrakanta* stone walls gave away the secret of this air-conditioning magic. The stone could absorb all the coolness of the moon and transfer it into the rooms. The stair walls were encrusted with diamonds and lined with gilded windows. The stairways had crystal flooring and ivory carvings on every landing. At even intervals in the hallways were gold pillars embellished with pearls, corals and diamonds. An intricately embroidered red carpet ran through the floor across the building, kissed by the best of tapestries that hung right from the ceiling. Every room looked rich and regal.

problem of plenty

As Hanuman continued to walk surreptitiously along the window railing, his sense of smell was overwhelmed by odors and aromas of different kinds. While some rooms smelled of flowers, others smelled of spice and drinks and yet some others smelled of exotic intoxicants. He could hear soothing music wafting out of several rooms. Hanuman realized that the ambience of the palace indulged all the five senses simultaneously. It was the most pleasurable experience any living being could aspire for in any lifetime. He felt he was in the heavens, perhaps an even higher level, if any existed.[30]

Of all the resplendent rooms, one stood apart. The intense level of activity far surpassed that of any other room. Hanuman's curiosity doubled when he noticed several gorgeous women sashay in and out of that room. So he hopped onto a vent above the room's massive door and peeped in. He wasn't sure if it was a dream. There were dozens of beautiful, angelic, unique women who seemed to have been brought from all parts of the universe. It seemed like a *stree vanam.*[31] Not all were involved in activity. Some were motionless as they were fast asleep. Some were half asleep. Some played their musical instruments, while some others merely held on to them. Some just sat listlessly on the carpeted floor still dressed in their best and most fashionable clothes. No matter what pose they were in, they all appeared drunk. The smell of liquor permeated the room. In their slumber, the women seemed like droopy lotus flowers that close at night. From the strewn flower garlands and jewelry, Hanuman understood that the room was witness to much more than just music and dance. The slumber smiles of some of the women perhaps reflected the pleasure they had experienced earlier. The huge room was full of beds teeming with intoxicated women in various stages of sleep.[32]

---

[30] One should be careful not to compromise one's character in retail while gratifying the senses in wholesale.

[31] Garden of women.

[32] That in which you marinate your thoughts becomes your reality.

In the sea of ordinary beds, Hanuman spotted a gigantic gold bed right in the middle of the room. It was studded with precious stones and had a white umbrella canopy, a luscious soft, sheepskin and silk bedspread, and four women in place of bedposts waving large silk fans to help circulate the fragrance from the celestial incenses. Hanuman noticed laying fast asleep on the bed among hundreds of women *the* person of interest: the mighty Ravana, the supremo of Lanka. The bright light from thc golden lamps next to the bed lent a golden glow to his lustrous body. Ravana resembled the moon among a sky full of stars. He looked as majestic as the Mandara mountain. His arms were like five-hcaded serpents. Rings made of precious stones of every color adorned his fingers. His thighs were as huge as that of elephant limbs. His shoulders bore victory scars from his innumerable military conquests. One such deep scar, Hanuman remembered from the legends he had heard, seemed like the one Airavata, the elephant of King Indra, had carved into the demon king with his tusks. Another deep mark near it seemed like the one caused by Indra's thunderbolt weapon. Hanuman also saw a gash made by Lord Vishnu's disc.

Ravana's listless body had smudges of the fragrant red sandalwood paste. On seeing a slumbering Ravana in all his splendor within his impressive palace, two thoughts crossed Hanuman's mind: If only Ravana had used his strengths to do some good in the world, he could have contributed so much. If only Ravana had been satisfied with the plenty he had, Rama would not have had to go through so much pain.[33]

---

[33] When people with impressive features carry out unimpressive actions, they receive very aggressive reactions.

As he wondered about Ravana's choices, Hanuman spotted another well-decorated cot with an angelic woman lying on it. She seemed to be of divine origin, quite different from the woman he had seen thus far in Lanka. Hanuman could see a pure and divine aura around her. *Could this be Sita?* Hanuman froze! He immediately began making a mental comparison between the woman on the cot and Lord Rama's description of Sita. It was an absolute match. *Finally!* Hanuman was ecstatic about having found Sita. He began to prance around kissing his tail, jumping, laughing and singing. Suddenly he stopped. Something didn't seem quite right. Hanuman regained his composure and began to admonish himself for even thinking that she could be Sita. He went over the description and cross-questioned himself on the gross error in his judgment. *How could Sita sleep in Ravana's bedroom? How could She sleep so peacefully in the absence of Rama? How could She be so decked up despite being away from Rama? When those connected to Rama never falter, how could I even imagine that His wife would? Even if gods like Indra or Kubera were to come, She wasn't the one to bend, so why would She even succumb to a demon like Ravana? Had She not rejected all the demigods and chosen Lord Rama, so why would She care to accept Ravana?* Hanuman was now convinced that only a disturbed mind seeks one that promises succor. Those under the refuge of Rama are secure enough and don't need to flit around. He resumed his search.[34]

Hanuman intensified his search and walked in and out of all the rooms in the palace he could. Everywhere he looked, he saw women in various stages of undress and sleep. He had to closely observe every woman he came across to ensure none of them was Sita. It was his job to find her from among all the women in Lanka. This was not something the celibate Hanuman wanted to do, but the job

[34] Looks may deceive, but mindsets will not ever.

had to be done. He began to question the righteousness of having to peep into homes and look at other people's wives, but his steady and pure mind justified his actions as having been carried out with no impure intent. He was conflicted about whether it went against his *dharma*. So he began to chant the name of Rama constantly to calm his disturbed mind. As the name of Rama permeated his being, he closed his eyes and a state of calmness spread all over his body. Clarity returned. *No, I have not come here with the intent of admiring Ravana's women. My goal is to find Sita among the women in Lanka. How can I search for a woman among deer? Besides, these women have not spotted me observing them and my mind has been steady and pure throughout this search.*[35,36]

Hanuman had scoured the entire palace and still not found Sita. He had observed more than twelve thousand women, and none happened to be Sita. He stepped out of the palace with a knot in his stomach and an ominous feeling swept his mind. *What if Sita isn't alive anymore? What if Ravana had killed Her? What if She had fallen into the ocean while being carried by Ravana?* Hanuman was so despondent that he wondered if he would ever be able to face anyone if he returned empty-handed. His bigger grief was the probability that there was no Sita left to find.

---

[35] Intelligence is the ability to balance faith and doubt.

[36] Chanting a *mantra* is like pressing the clutch. It gives you the freedom to change the gear of your mind from a state of disturbance to a state of peace.

Four Reasons for Valmiki's Detailed Description of Lanka

In the *Ramayana,* Valmiki describes the kingdom of Lanka in detail. Four reasons justify such lengthy descriptions.

1. To imply that the night was moving very slow and that the search was an excruciatingly and painfully slow one for Hanuman.
2. To compare Ravana with Rama. Ravana was a strong opponent and because of it he was a worthy enemy of Rama. It was important to describe the enemy elaborately so that people could appreciate the hero even more.
3. To show that Hanuman wasn't affected by either the opulence of Lanka or the temptations of women.
4. To show the stark contrast between *kama* or lust and *prema* or love. This description shows the difference between the purity and the great sacrifice found in real love and the decadence and abuse that is part of lust. What Ravana has for Sita and his wife Mandodari is lust, which involves no sacrifice or control. What Rama feels for Sita is real love, which does not hesitate to make boundless sacrifices.

Chapter 3

Garden of Despair and Hope

the domino effect

A tired, desolate Hanuman sat under a tree in a lonely section of Ravana's palace courtyard to recoup and re-chart his course of action. The futile search across Lanka and the combing operation had been grueling and a mentally draining experience. He had found the last phase quite intense and disheartening, so much so that he wondered if Sita had passed away. He began to recall all that he had been told before embarking on this mission and all that had happened since. *Was Sampati wrong after all? Even if he were, would Lankini also have erred in hinting about Sita's presence in Lanka and his success in this mission? Could anyone possibly survive in this highly secure place under the constant threat of Ravana? Was it possible that Ravana swallowed Sita in a fit of fury when She refused to succumb to his desires? Did Ravana's wives kill Her out of jealousy? Was it possible that Sita could not survive the pangs of separation from Rama? Or, did Ravana throw Her into solitary confinement into some cage in an inaccessible part of Lanka?*

The flurry of queries in his mind made him extremely anxious.

All sorts of defeatist thoughts began to flood his mind. The consequences of returning with no information about Sita's whereabouts were not lost on him. He knew that the very thought of losing Sita forever would kill Rama. Rama's demise would mean Lakshmana's end. Bharata would never be able to survive the news of Rama and Lakshmana's deaths. Shatrughna would naturally not live if his brothers died. With the demise of four sons would come the end of the three mothers. If every member of the royal family were to die, the citizens of Ayodhya would crumble. Unable to bear the guilt of being of no help to a friend who did so much for him, Sugriva would die. His death would take the life of Angad. Then Tara and Ruma would not survive the loss of their loved ones. And on seeing their king and prince dead, the entire *vanara* clan would exterminate itself. Hanuman could see a whole world of disaster in the face of one bad news: the total extinction of two entire races. His thoughts veered toward the suicidal. He thought it better to perish than to be the bearer of bad news.[1]

Once the whirlwind of agitated thoughts subsided, Hanuman began to think more logically. *Only cowards give up their lives. Life is a mix of good and bad days. Giving up during bad days is easy, but patiently waiting for the tide to change to herald good days is difficult. To see the good days, one must live. Enthusiasm is the foundation of progress. One who loses courage and cheer in life never tastes success.* The positive self-talk encouraged Hanuman to lift his head and look ahead. Suddenly, he spotted a beautiful garden he hadn't even noticed

---

[1] Hanuman was fine for as along as he was doing things, and he was not worried. But as soon as he sat down, worries began to take over.

Engagement is the antidote for worry.

Idleness is the free password to connect to the worry network.

so far. *How could such a huge landmark escape my attention? Hope, after all.*[2]

Before he set forth toward the garden, Hanuman folded his hands and offered a small prayer. This was a crucial night in Hanuman's life. *If this night were taken out of my life, my entire existence would be devoid of meaning. This night is my only chance to prove myself and serve Lord Rama in the most tangible way. There is no room for negativity tonight*. A silent prayer emerged from the deepest core of his heart. [3]

namosthu raamaaya salakshmanaaya
dhevyai cha tasyai janakaathmajaayai
namosthu rudhrendhrayamaanilebhyo
namosthu chandhaarka maruthganebhyah

[I offer my respects to Rama and Lakshmana. I then offer my respects to Sita, the daughter of Janaka. It is purely by Your grace, O Divine Mother, that I will be able to see Your divine form. I offer my respects to Rudra, Indra, Yama, Vayu, the god of directions, Surya and Chandra; all of you please help me find Sita.]

---

[2] Cheerfulness during tough times is the sign of acceptance.

Rather than looking at the descent from good days to bad days as linear, one should start looking at the transition as cyclic.

Enthusiasm is the chemical that keeps the milk of life from turning sour.

[3] What Hanuman did in one night got him the greatest celebration. Life gives you one chance to become a hero. Of course, that chance is never easy. People like Hanuman not only recognize that chance but also put in their best efforts toward not allowing negativity to demoralize them. They do not allow their mind to succumb to temptations. The world worships Hanuman due to what he did on this one night.

Verse to Find That Which Is Lost

According to the acharyas, the *shloka* or verse Hanuman chanted before looking for Sita in Ashoka *vana* supposedly helps regain what is lost.

Hanuman seeks the blessings of various divine entities to help him in his mission of finding Sita. Although he had begun his journey by seeking refuge in prayers, during his mission he had completely forgotten to depend on higher powers and relied on his own intelligence and strengths. Now on reaching a stage of hopelessness, he realizes the need to take shelter yet again.

He had promised the *vanaras* that he would go to Lanka like an arrow released from Rama's bow. However, on reaching Lanka and since the ensuing flurry of activities, it was only now that he sought Rama's shelter and focussed on Him.

Earlier too, when he was about to set out on his journey, he had offered respects to the gods and chanted the names of Rama. However, he hadn't offered his respects to Sita. This time he realized that without Her blessings, it was impossible to see Her.

Furthermore, each god he prays to represents the different virtues needed to find Sita.

1. Agni is fire and is symbolic of our *dharmic* or *daivic* thoughts. One needs divine thoughts to accomplish a divine mission.

2. Vayu is air and symbolizes *prana* or the most important part of one's life or that which is life itself. This represents our priorities.

3. Indra is the king of the heavens and is representative of *vajrapani* or strength of body and mind. To succeed in any mission, one needs the strength of both body and mind.

4. Varuna is water and internally represents *niti* or principles. Without integrity to higher principles, nothing big can be accomplished.

5. Chandra is the moon and stands for *soman* or the desire to live without deviating from *dharma*.

6. Aditya is the sun and symbolizes the *atma chaitanya* or will to live with integrity according to *dharma*. The *atma chaitanya* that is a witness to all our actions is *aditya*.

7. Ashwini *kumaras* are the twin demigods in charge of medicine who take care of *adhi* and *vyadhi*. *Adhi* implies diseases related to the mind, and *vyadhi* implies diseases related to the body. Most physical ailments are caused by the diseases of the mind. The Ashwini *kumaras* cure both. Now that Hanuman's mind is diseased with negativity, he needs their help.

8. Maruts are Indra's assistants who stand for *chintana shakti* or the ability to have deep thoughts.

Along with seeking the blessings of these divine beings, he also offers his respects to Sugriva, his master, knowing that it is only right and respectful to take into confidence and be blessed by an immediate superior.

a ray of hope

After offering this prayer, he shrunk to an even smaller size. Taking one big leap, he shot out like an arrow from a bow and landed straight inside the precincts of the garden, which he learned was

Ashoka *vana* or *vatika* or the garden of *ashoka* trees. As it was also a place where no *shoka* or lamentation existed, it was named *ashoka*.

Hanuman noticed the immense beauty of the garden, its multihued flowers, ponds with clear shimmering water, gold platforms and pearl-studded steps. From every direction, the garden seemed to be in a valley between several mountains with beautiful cascades. Caves dotted the raised landscape. The garden was filled with exotic animals, melodious birds, extraordinary flowers with exquisite fragrances and trees with tiny bells that chimed at every gentle nudge of breeze. Hanuman continued his search, careful to avoid being spotted by the *rakshasis* guarding the garden. He was astounded by the absence of male guards anywhere in the entire garden complex.

As Hanuman jumped from tree to tree for a thorough search of the garden, he startled the birds whose fluttering wings shook the flowers of the branches. The flower rain filled the garden with a million fragrances. Hanuman was covered with petals, and as he made his way through the garden, his presence unsettled the Lankan animals, too. The garden creatures thought he was the lord of spring.[4]

Hanuman ignored the animals and carried on with his search. The deeper into the garden he wandered, the surer he became of Sita's presence there. He even began to picture the spots She would go for Her bath and for Her oblations to the sun. He imagined which *ashoka* trees would remind Her of Rama and of Her stay at Panchavati. Just as Rama had asked the *ashoka* trees in Panchavati about Sita's whereabouts, Hanuman thought he could also ask the

[4] Ashoka *vatika* welcomes the great devotee Hanuman with flower showers.

ashoka trees in this *vatika* about Her, too. The possibility of finding Sita filled him with excitement and hope.[5]

Suddenly, a little distance away, Hanuman saw a golden tree. *How could a tree be made of gold?* Curiosity got the better of him, and he began to walk toward the mystical tree. As he inched closer, he realized that the golden luster was merely the reflection of the golden platform around the tree trunk. Even the steps leading up to the platform were of gold. It wasn't the usual Ashoka tree, but a *simshupa*[6] tree.

Hanuman climbed up the tree for a bird's eye view of the entire *vatika*. He was dying for a glance of Mother Sita. Since the beginning of the mission over two months ago, especially when the search was difficult, whispers and doubts among *vanaras* had grown louder. *Why were millions of vanaras engaged in the search of one woman? Was she so important that millions had to stake their lives and spend so many months in dangerous wilderness?* Standing on that *simshupa* tree, those doubts played on in Hanuman's mind.[7]

Just then he heard a sniffle. It seemed as if someone was sobbing. Hanuman's ears perked up and his head swiveled in all directions almost simultaneously. He had to locate the source of that barely audible sound wave that had come and gone. *There it was again!* Hanuman realized that the sound was coming from nowhere else

---

[5] The dish of life tastes best in the vessel of excitement and with a sprinkle of hope.

[6] Rosewood.

[7] When one is plagued by doubt, one can choose to either ask or wait. If one asks the right person, one will get the right answer, and if one waits for the right time, too, one will get the right answer.

but right from beneath where he was perched. He looked down and saw an extraordinarily beautiful woman in wrinkled and soiled yellow attire. He hadn't noticed her when climbing the tree as she was on the other side of the broad trunk. She had the aura of a *tapaswini*[8] and looked frail and emaciated. She appeared like a blazing flame amid smoke or perhaps a castaway treasure. A constant stream of tears rolled down from Her lotus petal-like eyes. She was surrounded by *rakshasis*, this delicate woman seemed like a fawn among hungry wolves.

He had a flash recall of a momentary glimpse of Sita during Ravana's flight over Kishkinda after abducting Her. He had seen Her throw a bundle of jewels at them. From the height he was at now, the form of the dainty woman being forcibly taken away quite matched the one below. This had to be Sita! This time he was certain. Not wanting to make a mistake yet again, he decided to observe Her more carefully to confirm Her identity.[9]

The divine woman was resplendent like the full moon. In fact, Her effulgence seemed to light up the otherwise dark Ashoka *vatika*. Her appalling condition notwithstanding, She had an undeniably regal demeanor. She resembled a slender sheet of gold-stained dust. Although apparently suffering, She seemed determined. Magnanimity oozed from Her persona. She seemed like the very

[8] A sagely woman.

[9] When Hanuman saw Mandodari, he acted like a typical monkey, but when he saw Sita, he was sober and expressed a lot of contemplation and thought.

Mandodari represents the false understanding of Sita.

Falsity always excites, and one ends up acting like a monkey. Truth is sobering, and one acts wisely.

mother of the universe. Her beauty far excelled even that of Rati, the goddess of love. She seemed to be tolerant like the earth itself. Yet She was sorrow personified. She had possibly reached the brink of hopelessness like someone who hadn't received the boons of a *tapasya.*[10] She exuded the helplessness and innocence of a newborn fawn. She had withered away in anxiety. She seemed like a warrior whose wound had healed but still concealed a small sharp splinter of an arrow within the wounded area, which was causing immense pain. It had been a long while since Her separation from Rama, but being away from Her beloved every moment seemed to cause Her extreme grief. She seemed like a tuft of cloud trying to re-merge with the bigger clouds it was forced apart from by a strong gust of wind.[11]

Hanuman noticed that the color and texture of the cloth matched that worn by the woman on Ravana's air carrier. In fact, a torn bit of Her attire seemed to match the cloth bundle She had flung at them on the Rishimukha mountains. He also noticed no jewelry on Her body. Instead, some pieces were hanging off branches. She may have flung those away in deep distress. He clambered down a bit to inspect the jewelry and realized that he had seen the exact missing pair of these in that cloth bundle back in the Rishimukha mountains.[12]

---

[10] Penance.

[11] Many wounds heal externally, but the pin that caused the prick remains embedded deep inside the consciousness and sends constant reminders of its hurtful presence in one's life.

[12] Observation before conclusion leads to clarity, and conclusion before observation leads to chaos.

finally, Sita!

Hanuman's descent down the tree matched the level of his surety – the surer he became, the more he descended from the tree. This time he hung low from the tree for a closer look at Her face. The flush of a warm smile spread across Hanuman's face. This was Sita, indeed! He leaned against the trunk of the tree and continued smiling blissfully. The smile was courtesy the first *darshan*[13] of Mother Sita.

His first impression was not unexpected. *Her facial features exactly match Rama's!* He realized that Her relentless focus on Rama had transformed Her enough to look like Him. Such was the power of Her mind and the highest form and the truest manifestation of Her love. Sita was separated from Rama physically, but She was constantly united with Him on a mental level.[14]

When he compared his dedication to Rama to that of Sita's, he realized he still had a long way to go. Hanuman's aim in life had been to only assist Rama, but after a glance of Sita and observing Her love for Rama, his goal evolved to develop that kind of uninterrupted love and service toward Rama. That instant Sita became his guru – the guru who taught him to develop true love toward Rama.[15]

---

[13] Glance.

[14] The acharyas explain that due to her constant meditation on Lord Rama's form, Sita had attained *sarupya mukti* – a type of liberation where the devotee attains the same form as the lord.

This is also seen among spouses who have deep love toward one another.

[15] Hanuman had called himself the messenger of Rama (*Ramadoota*), but after this incident he decided to call himself the servant of Rama (*Dasoham Kaushalendrasya*). *Sundara Kanda* of the *Ramayana* is Hanuman's journey from being *Ramadoota* to *Ramadasa*. This is a journey from an associate to a loving servant.

Hanuman thought that when he had seen someone in Ravana's bedroom that resembled her, he had felt nothing. But when he saw the real Sita, his each pore became alive. He had the same bone-melting experience now as he had on meeting Rama for the first time. He felt overpowered and overwhelmed. He felt sheer gratitude for Lord Rama in making him the instrument of His search for Sita. On seeing Sita, his mind rushed to offer reverence to Rama. Hanuman realized that he had never experienced as much love for his mother as he did for Mother Sita. He was dying to roll at Her feet like a little baby. He felt his life was perfect just on seeing Her. He suddenly developed a desire to be called "son" by Mother Sita.[16]

He had wondered about Rama's obsession with Sita and His loss of mental peace upon losing Her. After catching a glimpse of Her, he sensed a complete change in his perspective. *How could Rama live without Her for such a long time? How could He even live for a single moment in Her absence?* The only reason both were still alive was because Their minds were united. The infinite troubles that Rama underwent for Her sake all seemed worth it – be it the killing of demons such as Viradha and Kabandha or the decimation of fourteen thousand demons in Janasthan or the slaying of Vali to seek Sugriva's help or the search of millions of *vanara*s or his jump across an eight-hundred-mile ocean. Every herculean task was worth it when done for Sita. Whatever Rama had done so far for the sake of Sita was completely justifiable even if it meant turning the world upside down. If Sita were put on one side of a scale and the entire planet with all its precious things on the other, the value of everything would be the same as a blade of grass. There was

---

[16] Humility is not about showing but about feeling.
One must first *feel* small and then *be* small. Hanuman felt like a child in the presence of Sita, therefore he took a very tiny form.

no doubt that the moment Sita glanced at Sugriva, his fortune skyrocketed.[17]

Hanuman heard Her sniffle again. He could not but notice the irony of it all – the harbinger of fortune and good cheer was in deep sorrow. He reflected on the power of time, which could even put such divine personalities through tribulations. She was immersed in sorrow in Ashoka *vatika*, the place of no sorrow, and loveless amid *ashoka* trees, which were dedicated to Kama, the god of love. She was not wearing any jewelry, but She wore the ornament of Her love for Rama. She was pale yet effulgent. Every inch of the *vatika* reminded Her more and more of Rama.[18]

Hanuman wondered. *What must have protected Her over the last ten months? Was it Rama's* dharma, *Janak's* karma *or Sita's* punya? As he wondered about the contradictions in Sita's life, he began to feel two extreme emotions at the same time: joy on seeing Her and sorrow on seeing Her unhappy.[19]

He noticed Her lips moving constantly. On reading Her lips, he realized that She was constantly chanting the name of Rama. His eyes moistened and tears rolled down his cheeks when he saw Her love for Lord Rama – unabated and intact even after months of separation.

---

[17] Both love and hate revolve around troubles. In love, one takes troubles, whereas in hate, one give troubles.

[18] Great stories are about great people facing great tribulations with great dignity.

[19] One is in an existential tug of war game between one's life and one's mind. When life pulls towards negativity, one needs to pull one's mind towards positivity.

Sorrow was Her constant companion. What else could it be, given that She was surrounded by demons who did not really make acceptable companions? Before hopping down to meet Mother Sita, Hanuman wanted to first assess the security arrangements around Her. What he saw was simultaneously scary and funny. There were hundreds of horrendous *rakshasis* all around Sita. Of course, maintaining a safe distance to give Her privacy, but close enough as to not give Her freedom. Each of the *rakshasis* could induce paralyzing fear just by glaring at someone. Some of them had only one eye and one ear. Some had no face, and their eyes and mouth were on their stomachs. Some had the faces of pigs or deer or tigers or goats or buffaloes or foxes. Some even had the faces of elephants, camels or horses. Some had human faces but the ears of other creatures. Some had no nose at all, yet others had horizontal noses or noses on their foreheads. Each had some strange feature distinct from the rest. But all had one thing in common. They all loved to stay intoxicated and yearned for fresh meat. Their bodies were smeared with blood. While Hanuman was peering down from the branch, they were all asleep, piled up on each other like a heap of rags. This was the last phase of the night. Hanuman realized it was the opportune time to present himself to the helpless captive Sita. Before dawn broke, he wanted to meet Sita and convey Rama's message to Her.[20]

---

[20] If one has to choose between an out-of-shape body and an out-of-shape mind, one must choose an out-of-shape body, because when the mind is in shape, the body will soon fall in shape, too.

the lusty king

Just as he was descending from the tree, he heard drumbeats. He immediately returned to the safety of the branch he was on and hid himself behind a leaf. His form was so tiny that the small leaf concealed him. The drumbeats grew louder and as did the other accompanying instruments. This chaos seemed to herald the arrival of someone very important. Hanuman peeped in time to see the entry of the majestic king of Lanka in all pomp and glory. It wasn't yet dawn, and the king of Lanka was on his way to Ashoka *vatika* even as the whole of Lanka was asleep. This could only imply that he was desperate to acquire Sita. It seemed as if he was irresistibly drawn toward the Ashoka groves. Hundreds of women, holding torches and fans flanked Ravana. Some carried vessels of gold filled with water, while some others held gem-studded jars filled with liquor. Some cradled soft bolsters. Between all these sleepy beautiful women, the sleepy-eyed Ravana appeared like lightning amid clouds. His greased body, perfumed with aromatic oils, shone in the light from the torches. Hanuman had earlier seen him sprawled across his massive bed. He had seemed impressive even then, but now he looked even more attractive in his regal white silken attire flowing with the wind. This demon could easily charm any female in the world.[21]

Even though there were numerous beautiful women around him, his eyes were transfixed on Sita, who was crying under the *simshupa* tree. As soon as Sita instinctively felt the lusty Ravana's eyes on Her, She pulled her knees tight to her chest to conceal Herself. Tears of helplessness and fear gushed from Her eyes.

---

[21] In great desperation, discrimination is lost.

Ravana raised his right hand and his entourage stopped abruptly as did the cacophony of the instruments. An eerie silence haunted the garden. The sleeping *rakshasis* woke up with a jerk from their slumber and quickly assumed their alert positions, startled by the king's surprise visit.[22]

Shamelessly, Ravana walked up to Sita and placed his foot onto the platform on which Mother Sita was seated. He placed his elbow on the knee of that raised leg, his chin on the palm of his hand. He flashed a lustful smile at Sita. That smile would have made any other woman swoon, but Sita was disgusted. Even after ten months of attempting to win Her heart, Ravana had not made any headway. His patience was waning, considering he had never tried so hard for anything in his life. In fact, he had never had to try at all. He had to simply desire and everything and everyone automatically succumbed to his needs. Most women in his harem surrendered themselves to him. Initially, when Sita had rejected his advances, he took it as a challenge. Her resistance served to whet his appetite. But even after months of cajoling and torture, She had not relented. His patience was being tested to the extreme.[23]

With all the love that he could muster, Ravana spoke to her. "My dear Sita, do not be afraid of me. Why are you hiding your beauty from me? By abducting you, I have not done anything wrong as per *rakshasa* dharma. According to our codes, abducting another's wife is considered righteous. I may have brought you here without your

---

[22] A prepared mind hides realities.

[23] Sita represents the *aatma* or the true self. Ravana represents the false ego. The self belongs to the Supreme Lord, but the ego claims it and holds the *aatma* in a firm grip. Real wisdom lies in the ego surrendering the self and itself to the Supreme Lord, else it invites its own ruin.

sanction, but I shall not touch you without your will. By now you must be aware that there is no life for you outside of Lanka. Just hold my hand, and you can enjoy life in my company to the fullest. Your youth is ebbing…while you still have your beauty and youth, make the most of it. O beautiful damsel, Lord Brahma must have stopped creating anyone beautiful after creating you, as he seems to have invested all his creative talent in fashioning you. Every limb of your body is so exquisitely beautiful that when I stare at it, my eyes are enslaved. Even when you are dressed in dirty rags, your beauty radiates and defeats everyone else's in my harem. I will trade each of my women for a single smile from you. If you accept me as your master, then I will offer the entire world to your father to rule over as he pleases. Rama is a useless person. He is a fig in comparison to me. He is not equal to me in anything, be it austerities, strength, wealth, fame or brilliance. He couldn't save his own kingdom from slipping away from his hands, how can you expect him to come all the way to an island in the middle of the ocean just to save you? I am not even sure if he is …"[24]

Ravana ended his speech abruptly and shuffled back by a yard. Sita had thrown a blade of grass at him. From what Hanuman understood of the entire episode, this wasn't Ravana's first visit nor was it Sita's first rebuttal. It wasn't the first time She had thrown the blade of grass either. It didn't seem to bother him at all, but the grimace on Her face did. She was meek and fearful just a while ago, and now She looked fierce. *What did that look on Her face mean?*

[To know more about the 13 reasons for her throwing grass, refer to Adopt Patience, Book 3 of The Ramayana Game of Life series.]

---

[24] One cannot create one's image by slaughtering another's. Creativity doesn't take place in a slaughtering house.

The Blade of Grass

Every time Sita threw the blade of grass in front of Ravana, she kept meditating on its different meanings. In this incident, she was focused on a story.

Indra, Vayu and Agni had become too overconfident of their powers. To curb their pride, Lord Vishnu took the form of a *yaksha* and approached them. Agni asked him who he was. The *yaksha* in turn asked Agni who he was. This angered Agni, who began to emit his fiery rage. He told the haughty *yaksha* that he could burn the whole universe with his fire. The *yaksha* simply threw down a blade of grass and asked Agni to burn it if he could. No matter how much fire Agni emitted, the blade of grass just wouldn't burn.

When he was exhausted trying his best, Vayu stepped forward and boasted about his ability to blow that grass out of the boundaries of the universe. The *yaksha* welcomed him to try his hand. Vayu huffed and puffed, but the tiny blade of grass did not move.

Finally, Indra stepped forward. Seeing the state of his friends, his confidence was already lost. The *yaksha* didn't even bother to test him. He just picked up the blade of grass and walked away leaving behind a flabbergasted Indra.

Sita remembered this story while She threw that blade of grass this time in front of Ravana.

"You think you are powerful and have managed to gain control over the whole world. But My Rama is so powerful that you will not be able to move even a small straw that He places on the ground." When Sita spoke, anger spewed from every pore of Her body. "If you consider yourself greater than Rama, why did you carry Me away during His absence? Is this how *rakshasa*s define bravery? Are you tempting Me with luxuries? Don't you know that I shunned all luxuries the palaces of Ayodhya had to offer to be with Rama. When I consider those to be lesser than this blade of grass, why do you think I would be attracted to the wealth of your kingdom?"

Ravana's face began to swell in anger. Hanuman smiled at his plight. *What a stupid person! Does he think he can tempt Sita – the incarnation of Lakshmi, the goddess of wealth – with wealth? Without Her grace, Ravana would not have acquired all this wealth in the first place. And now by offending Her, he was going to lose everything including his life.* As Sita continued chastising and advising Ravana, Hanuman could see that She had taken the role of a mother correcting Her erring naughty child.

"Your desire to acquire Me is like a sinner aspiring for grace. Focus your mind on all the wives that you have, rather than lust after those out of bounds. Is there no one in Lanka that can drive some sense into your head? If you do not rectify your actions and lifestyle, you will soon be destroyed along with all your tribe. You can never separate Me from Rama just as light can never be separated from the sun. In your best interest, I advise you to reunite Me with Rama. If you surrender to Rama, He will surely spare you. Hold his hand and accept His friendship. He is kind and forgiving. But if you do not take Me to Rama, your death is certain. Rama's anger is more frightening than Indra's thunderbolt or Yama's noose. If you do not release Me now, you will soon have to face millions of arrows showered from the bows of Rama and Lakshmana. You must know that you are nothing but a barking dog next to the two tigers, Rama and Lakshmana. You are vain about your valor. I had noticed vanity when you abducted Me. You were no better than the petty thief who robs the house when the owner is away."

Why Hold Rama's Hand and Not Fall at His Feet

The acharyas explain that Sita knew the mood of Lord Rama very well. Rama always considered anyone who fell at His feet to be His friend. Be it Guha or Sugriva or anyone else, once a person fell at His feet, he became Rama's friend. Moreover, Sita contemplated that if Ravana were to surrender and he ended up touching Rama's feet, Rama would be upset that Sita had told a king to fall at His feet. He would surely have considered that inappropriate. Thus, understanding Rama's perspective, She told him to take hold of Rama's hand instead.

Ravana began to tremble in anger. Hanuman could see that his hands were itching to draw his sword out and slash Her. "Remember, you have only two more months to surrender." It seemed like he had allowed Her one year before submitting Herself. "If You don't, I will have you for breakfast."[25]

Sita scoffed at his comments. This time when She spoke, She was livid. "You, foolish man, as you say such lofty nonsense, death is sniffing you out. No one in all the three worlds would dare to speak to the Wife of Lord Rama the way you just did. Sadly, there is no one in Lanka who can advise you. By now your eyes should have popped out of their sockets for merely staring at Me with lust. Your tongue should have fallen out for uttering such wicked words. I could have easily burned you to ashes with the power of My purity alone. But I

[25] Those who are used to rejection don't accept themselves easily. Those who are used to acceptance don't allow others to reject them easily.

chose not to because it's only right that My husband be the one to punish you. Do not make the mistake of believing that I am a helpless woman under your subjugation. You speak such ignoble things about My husband and underestimate Him, but you will soon see His valor when he severs your head with His sharp arrows. What kind of a hero steals a woman by tricking her husband away?"[26]

Hanuman was on the edge when he saw a very incensed Ravana pull out his sword to chop Her head off then and there. Just at the nick of time, Dhaanyamalini, a beautiful woman, who seemed to be one of his several wives, grabbed Ravana's arm. She tried to pacify him. "Remember, master, those hundreds of celestial women who willingly succumbed to your desires. Of what use is this wretched and ordinary human to you? It does not suit someone of your stature to grovel this way in front of a plain woman who does not want you when you can be so happy with the many celestial women who are ever at your beck and call." The ego-pampering seemed to calm the demon king enough to stash away his sword.

"Increase the torture from this moment on and keep escalating it till she succumbs to my desire. Use any and every method at your disposal, be it *saama*, *daana*, *danda* or *bheda*. Do what you must, but I want quick results." Ravana hollered to the *rakshasis* on guard and left Ashok *vatika* glaring at Sita.

torture and tears

As soon as Ravana left, horrendous *rakshasi* women of all kinds closed in on her. The body odor of one of these women was so

[26] From the greatest helplessness emerges the greatest courage.

obnoxious that it could knock out anyone. Hanuman, the quiet witness, squirmed with anger every time Ravana spoke to Sita. Now seeing these *rakshasis* around Her was too much to bear with patience. All he wanted to do was pounce on them and pound them to pulp. But he had to hold himself down or risk jeopardizing this entire mission. He swallowed his anger and suppressed his urge to destroy the *rakshasis* and waited patiently for the right opportunity.[27]

A *rakshasi* Ekajata, who had a single strand of spiky hair bundled up on top of her head, spoke first. She admonished Sita. "You, foolish girl, don't you know that Ravana is the celebrated son of Vishravas, who was born from the thought of Pulatsya *rishi,* who in turn was the fourth Prajapati son of Lord Brahma?

Another *rakshasi* Harijata, with cat-like eyes that rolled in the sockets when she was angry, added her bit. "Don't you understand what a fortune it is to be the chosen wife of someone who has trounced not only all the demigods but their king as well?"

Yet another *rakshasi* Praghasa tried to flash her sharp teeth and intimidate Sita. She was more direct in her approach and gave no reasons. Instead, she asked, "Why won't you become the mighty Ravana's wife?

---

[27] While he jumped across the ocean, Hanuman was desperate not to waste any time. He didn't even wait for one moment at Mainak mountain. But now, inside Lanka when Sita was right in front of him, he was patiently waiting for hours for the opportune moment.

This shows the completeness of Hanuman's personality. He knows when to fight and when to fold, and he knows where to exhibit urgency and where to exhibit patience. Both a sense of urgency and patience are excellent qualities that a spiritual aspirant needs to possess. But more importantly, one should know where to exhibit which quality.

Vikata, another *rakshasi* was just as direct. "When Ravana himself has come to you and is dying to unite with you, why would you not consider his proposal?"

Durmukhi, a seemingly kinder demoness, took the justifications further. "The elements of nature are so afraid of Ravana. The sun exhibits heat that is proportionate to Ravana's desire to experience it. The wind blows to his liking. Trees shower flowers as he walks under them. Clouds disperse water only when and where he wants. When someone who has such control over the universe is so willing to be controlled by you, why would you not accept his offer?"

Sita couldn't care less about their praises for Ravana. In fact, the more they tried to convince Her, the more She felt irked by their presence. She just wanted to be left alone. Wanting to shut them up, She said, "No matter how much you try to convince Me, My mind is steady and won't change its ways. Even if all of you eat Me up piece by piece, nothing will ever change. I belong to Rama and no one else. Just as Sachi belongs to Indra, Arundhati to Vasishta, Rohini to Chandra, Lopamudra to Agastya, Sukanya to Chyavana, Savitri to Satyavan, Keshini to Sagara, Damayanti to Nala, Sita belongs only to Rama."[28]

This infuriated the *rakshisi* gang. They raised their weapons and aimed it at Her. Vikata roared. "This woman does not deserve to live anymore. When she is getting a chance to be the mistress of seven thousand women in Lanka, why is she being so adamant about being chaste?"

Chandodari, a *rakshasi* with a spear in her hand, spat out. "When we

---

[28] Loyalty that changes with situations is nothing but convenience.

cut this damsel, I reserve rights over her spleen, the soft flesh above her heart and a bit of her heart muscles and bits of her intestine."

Seeing everyone drool on hearing the names of so many of the tastiest body parts, Pragasa said, "If we have decided to finish her off, then why the delay? Let's just strangle her to death. Once we inform the king of her death, he will naturally permit us to enjoy the flesh.

When the situation seemed to become uncontrollable, Ajamukhi said, "Let us all divide equally and share our meal," to ensure she too had her share in the meal.

The wickedest of them all Surpanakha, who wasn't visible so far, suddenly stepped into the discussion and chipped in. "What Ajamukhi says is best. Let's divide her equally and relish the taste of fresh flesh. Let liquor be brought. With the best of eateries and the best of drinks, let us dance for the pleasure of our goddess Nikumbila."[29]

When Sita heard of these cruel and ghastly plans, She broke down. Not in the wildest of Her imaginations had She ever thought of finding Herself in this situation. She had no idea what to do. As tears rolled down Her cheeks, She folded Her palms and began to pray to Her deities. "O Rama! O Lakshmana! O Kaushalya! O Sumitra! Like a small ship in the middle of the raging ocean, I am being tossed around by the storms. What I am going through now

---

[29] Cruelty needs planning but compassion needs feeling.

Most people who think they give light to the world also end up giving a lot of heat to the world. Although the world needs the light of knowledge, it could do without the heated ego fights.

may be the result of the sins I may have committed in my previous lives. I do not wish to live anymore in this sinful place inhabited by mad people."

Sita rolled on the ground and began to weep incessantly. "Without Rama, there is no use of living. I will not even touch Ravana with My left foot, let alone desiring him. Even if I am cut into pieces, thrown into the blazing fire, or treated in any other way, I will never surrender to the whims of that demon. I know My Rama is compassionate and wise. I know for sure that He could never become hard-hearted and forget Me. But I do not understand why He hasn't come to My rescue yet. When He could kill a demon like Viradha to protect Me, why hasn't He come to save Me from Ravana? Has Rama died in the grief of separation from Me?"

voice of reason

"WAIT!"

Hanuman noticed that the loud shriek halted the clamor and chatter instantly. The voice was very loud and authoritative. He realized that everyone in Lanka could identify the voice of Trijata, the Ashoka *vatika* in-charge. She was the daughter of Vibhishan, the younger brother of Ravana. She interrupted the *rakshasis* who were amid serious discussions about their breakfast. Even Sita, who was praying intensely and lamenting about Her plight, stopped momentarily upon hearing the loud call.

Trijata stood up and stretched her arms above her head and walked toward the gaggle of *rakshasis*. She had been sleeping until quite late that morning. She had even managed to sleep through the commotion of Ravana's visit. Of course, as Ravana's favorite niece, she had many liberties. It was perhaps quite likely that Ravana noticed her sleeping and did not say anything considering she was just a child to him. But Trijata was no small child. She was intelligent and clairvoyant and was far superior to the regular *rakshasis*. Although she was much younger than most, Ravana gave her special privileges and even special responsibilities, including the supervision of his favorite garden.

"I just had a dream!" Her large eyes widened as she spoke. "A morning dream that is never untrue, a dream that will make you tremble in fear. Lanka's future is in jeopardy! Stay away from Sita and forget about eating her, eat yourselves instead. Worry for your lives."

The *rakshasis* became alert and were intrigued by her sudden declaration. "Tell us about this dream of yours. What did you see?" They seemed to taunt her. Even Sita was all ears. The tiny Hanuman, who had done a good job of merging with the foliage, too, perked his ears. So much had happened under the tree in the last few hours that he, too, was curious to know what a dream could possibly foretell about the future of Lanka and Sita.

Trijata realized that she had managed to capture their attention completely. "It wasn't just any dream. It was a revelation. Almost like a vision of the future unfolding. It sent tremors through my spine and every hair on my body stood erect while having those visions. I saw her husband Rama. He was wearing a beautiful white garland and was dressed in spotless white clothes. I am not sure what form of transport it was – a palanquin or a plane drawn by thousand white swans – but I do know for sure He was with His brother Lakshmana. I then saw Sita who was also in silken white clothes, seated on a white mountain surrounded by the blue ocean.

Suddenly, I saw Rama on a giant elephant with four tusks. Rama came on that elephant to the mountain and carried Sita away with Him. Sita who was seated on the lap of Rama, who was atop the majestic royal elephant, headed skyward and touched the sun and the moon with her hands. I then saw Rama, Sita and Lakshmana ascend onto the *pushpak vimana* and travel northward. Thus far the dream was fine. At least it wasn't negative. But the next phase was as bad as it could get.

I saw our master, Ravana, fall off the celebrated *pushpak vimana*. He was wearing blood red clothes and drinking oil. His head was shaved, and he was behaving like a lunatic. He was laughing and dancing like a mad man with a bottle of oil in his hand. He climbed into a chariot drawn by donkeys. The chariot began to fly toward the south as soon as he mounted it. Suddenly, he fell off the chariot, his clothes ripped off and he was naked when he fell to the hard ground. The naked, mad, awful smelling, slurry voiced Ravana entered a dark hole that sucked him in as he screamed endlessly. His brother Kumbhakarna followed him in another chariot drawn by camels. And then Indrajit followed suit in a chariot drawn by porpoises. I only saw my father Vibhishan treated differently. He was wearing white garlands and was dressed in royal clothes. His body was anointed with various essences and fragrant pastes. A white umbrella was held high above his head. He suddenly began to fly skyward with four other ministers.

I then saw the golden city of Lanka in ruins. The gates were broken down, and the arches had fallen into the ocean. I saw Lanka in flames. A *vanara* was prancing around everywhere, and it was smiling as the city burned. Just see! As I speak these words, look at Sita's left arm." Everyone turns toward Sita. Indeed, Her left arm was trembling. Trijata continued, "Look at Her left thigh!" Everyone noticed Her left thigh trembling, too. What did that even mean? The *rakshasis* wanted to know. They had no clue about the science of omens in which Trijata was a specialist.

"It just means that right now, Rama is very near Sita in some form." Trijata declared.

No sooner than she made the declaration, a *pingalika* bird cried. Trijata's jaw dropped at the sound. "This only confirms my theory. The bird is a harbinger of auspiciousness. The fact that it is perched on the tree under which Sita is seated and that it cried the moment I mentioned that Rama was present in some form around Her means that I was right. Lanka's destruction is certain. Sita, You need not worry anymore, Your husband Rama will very soon come and rescue You."

Half a Dozen Birds with a Message Each

On six different occasions in the *Ramayana*, six different birds convey six different messages.

1. The *Ramayana* begins with the *krouncha* bird being shot by the hunter, which inspires Valmiki to compose the first *shloka* of *Ramayana*.

2. In Kaushalya's palace, the *mynah* Sarika urges the parrot Suka to bite the foot of the cat to prevent it from taking the offerings to the deities.

3. In Panchavati, Jatayu fights with Ravana to prevent him from taking Sita.

4. On the shore of the ocean, Sampati revives the hope of the *vanaras* by pointing the exact location of Sita.
5. The *pingalika* bird, sometimes called the *vanjula* bird, assures Sita in Lanka of the coming of Rama.
6. During the Rama–Ravana war, Garuda comes just in the nick of time to save Rama and Lakshmana from the *nagastras*.

In each of these situations, the birds come at the right time to help avert a crisis. These birds represent the sages or wise and spiritual men.

There is great similarity in between a bird and a sage. Just as the birds fly high across the vast skies, the sages fly high through the vast experience of godliness. Just as the bird flies because of its two wings, the sages fly on the twin wings of knowledge (*gyana*) and practice (*sadhana*). Just as the bird rests on the branches of trees, the sages rest on the various branches of the *Vedas*.

restless future

Trijata's prophecies shocked and rattled the *rakshasis*. She was one of them and was their leader. They could not fathom what it all meant. They were not at all sure if they ought to believe in some stupid dream. None agreed or disagreed, but they all knew they were disturbed by whatever they had heard. They suddenly lost all interest in eating Sita. They did not even want to carry on with their discussion about Her. So they just left Sita alone with Her thoughts and went their different ways. They thought it best to calm their frayed nerves with intoxicants to numb all senses and sleep all their worries away.[30]

As the *rakshasis* floated into deep slumber, Hanuman's overactive mind was busy analyzing the events he had just witnessed. He was impressed by what he had just seen in the heart of Lanka. It was almost like a divine intervention in the most unexpected and most unconventional way. After witnessing this magic, his faith increased manifold.[31]

Hours passed, and Hanuman noticed that Sita could find no peace. Ravana's tormenting words and his warning kept ringing in Her ears. The taunts of the *rakshasis* kept replaying in Her head. Trijata's dream did fill Her with hope, but it was after all just a dream. She perhaps wondered how much faith She could have in a *rakshasi*'s dream. As the day passed, Sita seemed to become more and more restless, pacing around, trying to arrive at a conclusion.

---

[30] Numbing the mind is sadly considered the easiest way to numbing the problems of life.

The *rakshasis* went off to sleep because they didn't know how to deal with problems. Whenever they came across problems they could not deal with, they drank themselves to sleep.

[31] Hanuman always thought that there was no divinity in Lanka and that no saints could exist in such a godforsaken place.

But when he heard Trijata's dream, he realized that when divinity had to reach somewhere, it could reach through anyone and anyhow. He also understood that saints could exist in Lanka as well. If God resides everywhere, godliness, too, must reside everywhere. Where God resides, saints, too, must be there. He was very happy to see a divine intervention in a place like Lanka.

Hanuman saw Her stand up and pull down a branch. She seemed determined to execute some plan She seemed to have harbored for a while. Hanuman panicked. She was fidgeting with Her long braid, and if She was about to do what he assumed She would, it would be…

Chapter 4

Words of Comfort

a moment of dark despair

...too late. These words triggered the panic button in Hanuman's mind. Too late was not something he could afford. He had to act fast and do whatever had to be done in split seconds. The last few minutes had been a total disaster unfolding an unexpected sequence of events.

Sita had been wailing incessantly, blaming Herself for all the mistakes She committed in life that brought Her to this tragic state of existence. She kept reprimanding Herself for being too attracted to a mundane golden deer when She had Rama, the most precious jewel of all, and for being extremely rude to Lakshmana and doubting a saintly brother-in-law's character.[1]

Hanuman had then seen Sita shake off Her sorrow by wiping away Her tears and walking back toward the *simshupa* tree with a look

[1] Repentance is the side effect of anger.

of determination in Her face. Hanuman remembered having that sinking feeling that She was about to do something drastic when he had noticed Her pull down a thick sturdy branch of the tree. But he had been unable to fathom what to expect until he saw Her twirl Her braid around Her delicate fingers and look upward at the branch. It was then that Her intent became clear to him. Panic spread like wildfire through his veins.

He had to stop Her before it was too late. The One they had been searching for months and the One for whom he had taken so much trouble to cross the ocean, was about to give up Her life.[2]

Her saw Her fling Her long braided hair over the branch She had been holding low with one hand. Hanuman could feel time slipping away as he saw Her tie Her hair as a noose around Her delicate neck and attempt desperately to make a knot with one hand while clinging onto the branch with another.

Before time froze forever, Hanuman had to make the most of the few seconds he had before She let go off the branch. Hanuman's mind hustled to arrive at the most appropriate plan under the circumstance, considering She had no idea if He was a well-wisher or an enemy. Hanuman's mind was a cacophony of questions that he was processing at great speed. *What if She thinks I am Ravana disguised as a* vanara? *She would then let go even faster. If a* vanara's *sudden jump in front of Her startled Her, She would involuntarily lose Her grip and be strangulated. What if She raised an alarm and all the rakshasis woke up? They would surely attack me, and I would miss the chance to convey Rama's message to Her. What would I report back to Rama and Sugriva then? That I met Her but failed to talk to Her? Or*

---

[2] No one struggles alone.

worse still that I watched Her as She took Her own life?

Hanuman shushed all the noise in his head, for the time to act was now. He had to do whatever it took to save Her life and save his own life and that of everyone else connected to this mission. *Words. There is great power in words!*[3]

Hanuman realized he could utter a few significant words and save the day. He knew he had to choose his words very carefully. Sita had, by this time, managed to tie Her hair to the branch. She was on Her toes now as Her hand was aching from holding the heavy branch, and She was slowly losing Her grip and the noose was beginning to tighten around Her neck.[4]

Hanuman had to frame pertinent sentences soonest and ensure that his words not only stopped Her from executing this drastic move but also provided Her hope and much-needed succor under the grim circumstances. There was no other solution than using words that would directly touch Her heart.[5]

As Hanuman was debating what to say and how to say it, Sita was having some interesting experiences of Her own. As the braid noose began to strangle Her and the branch began to spring upward, lifting Her up in the process, She began to experience some divine omen all around Her. Her left eye began to twitch, and Her left thigh began to shiver. Her left arm also began throbbing. She saw auspicious signs

---

[3] Words can either set you free to fly in the sky or bury you deep to die in the grave.

Words can often lift heavy burdens to lighten the spirit.

[4] A good thought is often a bridge between living and dying.

[5] The language of the heart has no script but great dialogues.

all around Her. She recalled having experienced all these omens together earlier, too. Even when in the most awkward situation of Her life, where She was dangling between life and death, She began to smile, surprising even Her own self. The smile was reminiscent of the last time She had experienced all these auspicious omens all at once: during Her wedding to Lord Rama. She began to wonder. *What do these signs mean now? Does it mean that I will be reunited with Rama after My death? Does it mean that I need not die because Rama will rescue Me soon as per Trijata's dream? Does it indicate some divine intervention?*[6]

that hopeful retelling of Her life

Sita's mind was flooded with conflicting thoughts, which became more complex because of the life-terminating decision She had made. As She tried to make sense of what was happening with Her, She heard a gentle, soothing and melodious voice that pierced right through Her heart. As soon as that voice entered Her ears, She felt compelled to close Her eyes. She wanted to experience that voice to the fullest by allowing it to flow to the deepest core of Her being. She could feel a strong affinity to the voice. *This is no ordinary voice. I feel a very deep connection to it.* She realized that even though this was the first time that She had heard that voice, She felt instinctively drawn to it.[7]

---

[6] Within inauspicious ends of life are often hidden the most auspicious beginnings.

[7] The deepest human connections are not of blood but of voice.
Such a deeply connected teacher and student are called voice mates.

Hanuman's Communication Deliberation

Hanuman had to weigh his options of communicating with Sita very carefully. He had multiple choices, and with each choice came consequences. His first option was to speak in Sanskrit, which is *deva bhasha* or the language of the gods. But then there was the possibility of Sita mistaking him for the polyglot Ravana, who also spoke the language of the gods. It might lead Her to wonder if Ravana had disguised himself as a *vanara* to deceive Her. The second option was to remain silent. Although silence would not create the confusion the wrong choice of language can create, it would not be possible to convey a reason for Sita to choose life over death. Hanuman decided the third option was the best. If he spoke the Awadhi dialect, Sita would immediately understand that it was someone near and dear to Rama. No one spoke or understood Awadhi in Lanka.

The depth of the voice, the modulation, the intonation and the language were all so dear to Her heart that it captured Her complete attention. Sita felt that the voice almost sounded like Rama's.

raja dasharatha naamah ratha kunjara vaajimanaam

Hanuman started by extoling Sita's father-in-law, Dasaratha. He said, "There lived a great King Dasaratha, who was a master in the art of chariots." The very mention of Her father-in-law and the dialect hooked Her right away.

Hanuman went on. "The great King Dasaratha was among the most glorious kings of the Ikshvaku dynasty. He was a great conqueror, but his greatest joy was the birth of his four sons. The eldest was Rama."

Sita could sense a distinct change in the tone. She could feel the deep love when the word Rama was uttered. It was the most amazing sound Sita had ever heard in Her life. That voice uttering Rama's name was sublime! She had to close Her eyes to completely immerse Herself in the feeling running through Her. She looked upward to ascertain where the voice was coming from, but She couldn't see anyone up there. A genuine kindness in the voice made it even more endearing to Sita.[8,9]

Hanuman continued to narrate Rama's story from the moment He was born to King Dasaratha and Queen Kaushalya. He also mentioned minute details of His childhood that even Sita did not know. He went on to describe the wedding ceremony of Sita and Rama almost as if he were present at the event. He even explained the subtle nuances and emotions of people present at the wedding.

Sita could hear great jubilation in the voice. Hanuman's voice quivered, cracked and choked as he narrated the rest of the story. "Rama was then exiled from the kingdom of Ayodhya, and all of Ayodhya wept." Sita could even hear sniffles. "The citizens of Ayodhya and the royal household experiencing gut-wrenching pain as Rama's chariot made its way out of the kingdom." Sita could not control Her tears as the voice took Her back in time and refreshed Her ordeal. The voice then narrated every detail about the thirteen

---

[8] This was the first Rama *katha* ever in Lanka. With this *katha*, Hanuman set the precedent of the speaker sitting on a raised platform and the audience at a lower level, making the exalted *vyas asan* a norm.

[9] Kindness cannot be shown but can be felt.

years of their exile, including Bharata's visit to Chitrakoot, Their life in Dandakaranya forest and the few years in Panchavati on the banks of the beautiful Godavari river. Sita smiled as She heard the voice talk about those thirteen years. She had considered those years spent in Rama's company Her best. The voice described everything, including the deepest of emotions in detail so Sita could relive Her love-filled days with Rama. As the voice continued tugging at Her heartstrings with its emotional intensity, Sita looked up to see if She could spot anyone there. But no one was there.

"The spat between the trio and Surpanakha was intense…fourteen thousand demons headed by Khara and Dushan had become a menace, and Rama put an end to their misery by annihilating the whole lot…a golden deer leaped into Sita's life. At Sita's insistence, Rama began to chase the deer…Soon Sita heard a voice calling out Her name and Lakshmana's, looking for help. She panicked and sent Lakshmana to look for Rama and was abducted." The voice then began to tell Her about things She had never known. She had known only Her side of what had happened, but this voice gave Her Rama's perspective and even Lakshmana's. Sita was once again filled with remorse about Her mistake. She silently begged forgiveness from Her brother-in-law Lakshmana for having humiliated him.

The voice went on to describe things that She had been unaware of until this moment. "Rama is in deep anguish and agony because of His separation from Sita. Rama kept begging all the animals and trees to tell Him about Her location. He went through so much pain and trouble while searching for His beloved Wife." Sita couldn't believe that Her sober self-controlled Husband could become nearly mad in Her absence. Hearing about Jatayu's death and his loyalty to Rama until his last breath broke Her heart. The voice continued.

"Rama walked miles and miles with Lakshmana in His quest for Sita and eventually met with the *vanara* Sugriva who rallied an entire army of *vanaras* to search for Her across the globe. Even as I speak, Sugriva's *vanaras* are spread across different corners of the earth searching for Sita." When Hanuman described the detailed combing operation, Sita was touched by the intense effort put toward finding Her. She had tears of joy and sorrow as She heard and lived the moments of Her life and that of Her beloved Rama and His brother Lakshmana.

Finally, Hanuman revealed about himself. "Then I, a swift *vanara*, on the suggestion of Sampati, have jumped over the eight hundred-mile ocean and overcome all the obstacles along the way. I have combed through every inch of Lanka and finally managed to find You here in Ashok *vatika* through the power of prayer. I have a message for You from Your beloved Lord Rama."

By then, Sita had unwound Her braid from the branch, let go off it and sat on the ground looking up to find the face behind the voice. She hadn't been able to see anyone speak, but the words had given Her such comfort and so much relief. Unlike the others who surrounded Her and gave constant pain, here was the voice of someone She hadn't even met or seen, who had crossed a huge ocean, trekked thousands of miles, and faced hundreds of challenges, just to meet Her. She offered Her respects mentally to that invisible well-wisher who had compassionately entered Her life.

She looked up and noticed some shuffling among the foliage. Then slowly one of the leaves bent, exposing a gap. Through that gap peeked a very charming and tiny *vanara*. Sita noticed that the innocent brown eyes staring at Her looked like the sun rising in the horizon. Just as the sun heralds hope, this little *vanara* had given Her newfound optimism.[10]

Just as She spotted him, Hanuman jumped off the tree and on to the platform with a soft thud. He folded his hands and held it above his head as a mark of veneration toward Sita. As he walked closer to Her, he morphed into an even tinier *vanara*. He exuded strength in his white garments and a yellow silken dhoti. He was barely up to Sita's ankles, but his body was well chiseled. He knelt on one knee and offered his salutations to Her. Sita almost felt tempted to call him "son" because of his miniscule tiny size but...[11]

Palms Folded

In Vedic culture, when one folds one's palms in front of someone, the palms are held at different levels depending on who that someone is.

In front of one's mother, the folded palms are at stomach level.

In front of one's father, the folded palms are held at neck level.

In front of one's guru, the folded palms are held at face level.

In front of God, the folded palms are held above the head.

When Hanuman appeared in front of Mother Sita, he held his folded palms way above his head showing Her the highest level of respect.

---

[10] Valmiki mentions here that Hanuman had revived Sita's desire to hear the glories of the Lord, which had been stolen by grief. This is the expertise of an acharya. He revives one's desire to hear about the Lord.

[11] Hanuman had taken on that tiny form just to evoke the word "son" from Mother Sita. He was dying to hear that word come out of Her mouth.

the test of devotion

The moment She saw the *vanara*, three doubts stormed Her mind. *Is this all a dream?* She could not imagine anything related to the *vanara* to be true. A talking *vanara* crossing the vast ocean and managing to meet Her despite Lanka's tight and exemplary security seemed too good to be true. *This sudden form change from an ordinary vanara to a vanara warrior is baffling!* He had taken a few steps to be closer to Her. Both the disguise and the advancement toward Her seemed like attributes of Ravana. *How could I trust him?* Sita's face then straightened and She suddenly became stern.

"Stop right there! O Ravana, you cannot fool Me with your *vanara* disguise! No matter what trick you try, I will not succumb to your evil intentions." Sita's sudden attitude change shocked Hanuman. He had no idea what had come over Her and caused Her to behave this way. He had thought everything through and used the most apt method to convey his message to Her. He had not anticipated this reaction, not after his chosen method of communication, at least. So Hanuman did what he thought was best at that moment. He raised his hands above his head and fell at Her feet. Although taken aback, Sita wanted to be sure that it wasn't one of Ravana's tricks. She was sure that Ravana would never do this. In the ten months that She had observed him, She knew that if there was a sure way of testing Ravana, it was this.

She looked at the tiny *vanara* warrior lying prostrate before Her and said, "Get up! If you really want Me to believe you to be My beloved Lord's messenger, you will have to pass a test. I want you to describe the form of My husband Rama. If you are indeed a messenger, I will easily know from your description."[12]

The little *vanara* hero smiled. She was telling him to do what he loved to do. He closed his eyes and meditated on the form of Lord Rama that he had first seen at the base of the Rishimukha mountains. But as he meditated on the form of Lord Rama and tried to formulate words to describe Him, all the letters and words he ever knew began to float inside his mind. He felt that if he compared Lord Rama's body with any beautiful object of this world, all other beautiful objects would become upset. But if he didn't speak at all, then it would upset Sita. For a moment, he thought crossing the ocean was easier than Sita's test. He took a deep breath and embarked on the impossible task.

"Radiant as the sun, refreshing as the moon, that divine emerald green body has a golden tinge. Even the god of love who mesmerizes people of this world faints upon seeing that resplendent beauty of my master Rama. With beautiful long lotus petallike eyes, red lips like the *bimba* fruit, a broad deep chest and a robust eight-feet tall physique, Rama enamors every heart that glances upon Him. He is the bliss that can be felt, experienced, seen and touched. His grandeur is like that of Kubera's, His prowess like Lord Vishnu's and His speech as wise as Brihaspati's. His dharmic views make Him the personification of *dharma* itself. His battle victories resemble Indra's.

---

[12] The acharyas explain that Sita wanted to hear more about Rama from Hanuman; therefore, She acted as if She considered him to be Ravana disguised as a monkey. The first time She heard him narrate a Rama *katha*, She couldn't see him. This time She wanted to hear the Rama *katha* seeing the speaker and thus acted as if angry.

His strength can protect the whole world. He has expert control over His desire and anger just as He has control over His chariot. Not only is He strikingly beautiful to look at, His virtues make Him extremely attractive and lovable, too. His positive attributes are as limitless as the clouds. All that is excellent in this world is embodied in Him. O Mother, you are asking me to extol His glories, but how can I feel I have said enough about His greatness when I know His greatness and qualities are infinite and my ability, intelligence, choice of words and time itself are finite."

Tears gushed from Her eyes like a stream. Sita was in the throes of such intense spasms of emotions that words failed Her. Her love for Rama increased upon hearing the *vanara*'s words of praise. "O best of the *vanaras*, please tell me more about My Rama and Lakshmana. How are they? How did they manage to forge a friendship with the *vanaras* although they are a different species?"

"Rama is perfection personified. Everything He does becomes the standard for perfection. Be it in statesmanship or *tattva gyana*[13] or good conduct or conducting fire sacrifices or archery skills or understanding the *Vedas*, Rama is simply perfect.

His broad shoulders, long arms, short neck, high collarbone and extremely handsome countenance all have raised the bar for attractiveness. His voice is deep, and His skin is so soft, silken and glowing. His limbs are in perfect symmetry. Rama has *saundarya*[14] and *lavanya*.[15] As I try to describe the beauty of one of His limbs, I feel compelled to describe the others.

---

[13] Knowledge of higher truths.

[14] This means that each limb of Rama's body is exquisitely beautiful.

[15] This means His overall beauty is mesmerizing.

My dear Mother, Rama and Lakshmana are one soul within two bodies. They are very similar in Their appearance and qualities. Their dedication to one another is unbelievable. Through all these tough days of separation from You that Rama experienced, Lakshmana stood by Him like a rock. The only difference between the two is Their complexion. While Rama's body is a gold-tinted emerald green, Lakshmana's is the color of molten gold." Hanuman was so excited and overjoyed to narrate how Sugriva and Rama met in the Rishimukha mountains with him as mediator. He told Sita of Vali's elimination and Sugriva's subsequent coronation. He also added elements of his own life to help Sita trust him. "You, Mother, are the real cause of the meeting between Lord Rama meeting Sugriva and their subsequent friendship." When Sita seemed surprised, Hanuman said, "Do You remember throwing Your jewelry bundled in a piece of cloth as You were being abducted? That bundle had landed directly at the feet of Sugriva, thus making him the chosen one. I was fortunate enough to be standing amid the five *vanaras* when the bundle landed. I had caught a glimpse of You at the time from a great distance. That moment when Your glance fell on the five of us, the destiny of the *vanaras* and the land of Kishkinda changed."

Hanuman continued as he brought the focus back to Rama's miserable state. "O Mother, please know that Rama feels like He's been tossed into a burning house. He constantly trembles in grief, tormented by Your loving memories. Sugriva has directed the *vanara* army to go in search of You in all directions across the world. But it is my good fortune that I became the one among the millions of my friends to have found You. My name is Hanuman, and I am the messenger of Rama and a servant of Sugriva. If You are wondering how I managed to achieve what millions of other *vanaras* couldn't, let me assure You that it has nothing to with my personal greatness. It is due to the power of a treasure that Rama had given me before

I embarked on this search mission. From the moment that treasure has come into my hands, my strength and wisdom have enhanced rapidly. I have acquired knowledge of things that I didn't even know of. I spoke to You of many things about Rama's journey and Rama's persona that I could have never known myself. By the power of this treasure, I could cross over an entire ocean with no exhaustion or fatigue. I went undetected as I traversed through such a secure kingdom just by the power of this treasure that I have in my hands."

The more She heard about Rama, the more She wanted to hear. This little *vanara* was speaking so well. He had the gift of Mother Saraswati on his tongue. Whatever he spoke sounded like nectar and was full of hope. She raised Her hands joined Her palms and expressed Her gratitude.

Hanuman stepped in front of her and held out his palms. Sita wiped away Her tears and tried to see what he was trying to display. She saw in his palms a beautiful golden ring. It had a red ruby and the name Rama embossed on it. Sita was so overwhelmed with emotion that Her tears would not stop flowing. This ring had been Her constant companion for so many years. She had worn this ring from the day She married Rama until the day They ferried across the Sarayu river. On that day, as a token of gratitude Rama had wanted to offer the boatman something valuable for ferrying Them. Noticing His need, Sita had offered to give this ring to the boatman. The boatman had refused. But Rama, rather than returning it to Her, had worn the ring. At that time Sita had felt it was unlike Rama to wear Her ring. But in retrospect, perhaps Rama knew back then that this ring would serve to unite Them in the future as it had in the past.[16]

---

[16] Behind every unusual action, there must be a story. Rather than discovering that story, people end up doing a post-mortem of the action itself.

"O Mother, You wanted to know how Rama is. The beauty of Lord Rama that I have described to You was true, but that was all before Your abduction. From the time You have been missing from His life, He has become so emaciated that this ring has now become an amulet for Him."

Hanuman held out the ring for Sita to pick it up. Hanuman thought it was perhaps inappropriate to give someone as divine as Her anything at all. But if She took from him what was rightfully Hers, that would be perfect. He did not want to harbor the pride of being a giver to Sita.[17]

As Sita held out Her hands to reach out to the ring placed on Hanuman's outstretched palms, Her arm began to tremble in anticipation. It was almost like reaching out to touch Rama. This ring had been in Her beloved's hand for years now. The first touch of the ring in Her fingers sent tremors of ecstasy through Her body. She held it close to Her face, examined the ring from all directions, almost as if admiring Her husband's face. She then held it to Her cheeks very intimately. Hanuman's description of Rama's condition had made Her feel extremely sad for Him. He had to go through so many tribulations for Her sake. She had promised to be His support in sorrow, but here She was so far away from Him. At the same time, Sita was happy that She had received the ring from Rama and learning that Rama missed Her too. It was such a relief. Her doubtful mind and the *rakshasis* of Lanka had aroused in Her the suspicion that Rama had perhaps forgotten Her. Sita shed tears of

---

[17] If Hanuman had to place the ring in Her hands, it would subtly indicate that he is superior to Her. But, by allowing Her to pick up the ring from his palm, he clearly indicated that he is inferior to Her.

Subtleness in behavior is indicative of depth of sensitivity.

joy and sorrow, wetting the ring. "Hanuman, your words are like nectar mixed with poison. While they have made Me happy, they have also made Me sad."[18]

Once Her emotional tide subsided, Sita told Hanuman a story only She and Rama knew. "One day, as I was sitting with Rama in Our private chambers, We had a friendly argument over something trivial. Somehow, while trying to pacify Me, Rama inadvertently rubbed off the vermilion on My head, which was the symbol of My marriage. I took it very seriously as I considered it inauspicious and told Him that it would bring Him harm. My concern for Him made Me cold, and I stopped speaking to Him. After a while, Rama also stopped trying to pacify Me, and it became a cold war. For days together, We did not speak to each other even though We were in the same room. It came to a point where none of Us wanted to be the first to initiate a conversation. One day, as I was seated on a swing, I began to think about ways to end Our cold war. That's when this ring gave Me an idea. I acted as if I dropped the ring by mistake on the floor and began to look for it without getting off the swing. Then I spoke loudly, ensuring that Rama had heard Me. 'Is there anyone here who can help Me find My lost ring?' Rama immediately jumped into action and found the ring. Handing it over to Me, He looked into My eyes and smiled. I had so missed His smile. I couldn't resist smiling back and that was the end of Our fight. This ring had united Us then, and it is uniting Us now."[19]

---

[18] Bad news should be given with a healthy padding of hope. Though the punch still hurts, it's bearable.

[19] In between people who love, fights are like toppings on the main meal of love for life to be tasty.

But when love becomes a topping on the main meal of fights then the taste of life gets spoilt.

Hanuman smiled. *How sweet is Their love!* Sita then began praising Hanuman. "How valorous you are and how loyal toward Rama. Your intelligence and presence of mind are exemplary. You must be the most special among the *vanara* clan for Rama to have chosen you to perform the task of crossing over the ocean to find Me."

Roles Reversed

Here Sita and Hanuman's conversation brings out the essence of the *guru-shishya* (teacher-student) relationship. Sita represents a qualified disciple and Hanuman the bonafide guru.

Before trying to connect with Her, Hanuman makes a thorough check to determine Her consciousness. Only when he notices Her fully absorbed in the agony of separation from Lord Rama does he decide that it's imperative to rescue Her. The bonafide spiritual master prioritizes that disciple who has the great eagerness to advance in spiritual life and reconnect with God.

Sita, on the other hand, does not accept Hanuman as Rama's messenger either without thoroughly testing him. Just because he says he is a representative of God doesn't mean that he is one. The test of a bonafide guru lies in his ability to describe the Lord. Unless he has understood and experienced God, he would not be able to describe God convincingly.

Only when both Sita and Hanuman are convinced about each other's genuineness does Hanuman hand over the ring. Only when the guru sees that the disciple is qualified, does the guru offer the symbol of God. In the different stages of being a disciple, the guru offers different symbols to establish the disciple's connection with God. This formal process is called initiation, wherein the guru formally connects the disciple with God.

In *Sundara Kanda* of the *Ramayana*, there are two very beautiful things. One is God's name and the other is God's *katha* or glories. Hanuman offers Sita the ring with Rama's name on it and he narrates Rama *katha*. Sita is in Ashoka *vatika* and praying for divine intervention to end Her *shoka* or lamentation. That is when Hanuman comes and offers Her Rama *nama* and Rama *katha*, which ends Her lamentation.

Sita is in Lanka where Ravana is willing to offer Her gold, but that doesn't impress Her at all. But when Hanuman gives Her the small golden ring, She feels so inspired and affected. That is the difference between love and lust. A little offered with love holds more value than a lot offered with lust.

After appreciating Hanuman profusely, Sita asked him a question that had been troubling Her. *If Rama is safe, if Rama is angry, if Rama has powerful weapons, if Rama loves Me, if Rama is capable, then why hasn't He come to rescue Me yet?*[20]

Up until he had reached Lanka and found Her, Hanuman explained that they had no confirmation about Her whereabouts. There was no possibility of rallying an entire army without a confirmed location to attack. Hanuman convinced Her that the moment he returned with the information about Her exact location, the *vanara* army would descend southward and vanquish the Lankan army.

[20] Helpless people always look out for understanding people.

heart-to-heart talk

Sita poured Her heart out to Hanuman. "My dear son, please inform Rama that Ravana had given Me a year to succumb to him. Only two months are left. If by the end of these two months, Rama does not rescue Me from the clutches of this demon, then I will be left with no option but to give up My life."

The painful words disturbed Hanuman so much that the very thought of it made him decide to do something right away. He stood up and told her, "O Mother! Come with me right now. Forget the two-month wait. Let's not wait even for a day. Please sit on my shoulders; I will carry You to Rama right now. There is no need to tolerate any more torture here."

Even amid a crisis, Hanuman's words made Sita smile. Hanuman was surprised to see Her smile, especially since he was making such a serious suggestion. Containing Her smile, Sita asked Hanuman a question. She didn't want to embarrass him but needed some clarity. Not wanting to embarrass him, She asked him, "Are all the *vanaras* of Sugriva's army the same size as you?"

She smiled again. The intelligent Hanuman immediately understood what She meant. Sita had wanted to know how a small *vanara* like him could boast of being able to carry Her on his shoulders to Lord Rama. Hanuman realized the question did not need to be answered.[21]

He closed his eyes and chanted the name of Rama repeatedly

---

[21] Insensitive people question, sensitive people inquire.

under his breath. As he chanted, his size began to increase. Soon, he was gigantic. Sita had to stand up to be able to even see his face, which was somewhere in the sky. He was much bigger than the giant *simshupa* tree under which She was standing. His sudden transformation surprised Her. She was quite used to the little monkey. Hanuman's new size raised another doubt in Her mind.[22]

"My dear Hanuman, what is your actual size? Are you small or are you big?"

This was becoming interesting. Hanuman realized Sita's questions had a direct and an indirect meaning. This question was more of a test. Hanuman replied in a way that really touched Her. He made sure that his reply came from deep within his core. "My dear Mother, I am very small and insignificant. But for the mission of the Lord, I can take any size. To serve Rama, I can do anything. I can carry the whole of Lanka with all its mountains and palaces and throw it at Rama's feet."

Sita was thrilled by that answer. He was not only intelligent and strong but also sensitive. She developed great motherly affection toward him. Hanuman resized himself such that his identity remained concealed from the *rakshasis* who were snoring away. Sita was impressed with him. "I can now understand the might of the *vanara* army just by looking at you."

[22] The purpose of life is to expand the horizons of one's contribution.

Much More Than Size

Size equals responsibility. When Hanuman says he can take any size for the mission of Lord Rama, he means that he can take any responsibility for His sake. Most people wrongly understand the concept of humility. They use false humility as a foil for their laziness. When given any responsibility, they shirk from it by calling themselves insignificant and unqualified. Hanuman, on the other hand, calls himself small but also makes it clear that he is quite capable of taking up bigger responsibilities and adapt accordingly. He knows well that although he is insignificant, the Lord can empower him to do things of great significance. Such dependence and faith are the real essence of true humility.

Hanuman prefers to keep himself small in front of Mother Sita. Even when he shows his huge form, he shrinks quickly and re-assumes his small size. This is because he wants Her to consider him as Her youngest son. The youngest child gets the most favor and love of the mother.

Those who are big are unable to become small because they are so proud. Those who are small cannot become big because they are incapable. But Hanuman can do both because he is not only humble but also capable.

Becoming small when you are big is *bhakti yoga*. Becoming big while you consider yourself small is *karma yoga*.

Hanuman spoke again. "O Mother, please know that everyone else in the *vanara* army is either equal to me or better. There is absolutely no one in the army inferior to me. You must be aware that kings only send their most insignificant warriors as messengers to an enemy camp. Please be assured that Rama's *vanara* army is well-equipped to rescue You. We don't even have to wait until the army comes here. You could just agree to get onto my back, and I could take You to Lord Rama right away. Please come with me right now."[23]

"No! No! I cannot come with you because I fear heights."

Hanuman laughed at Her reasoning. "My dear Mother, Ravana too brought You through the skies. Now that You have a chance to return to Rama, could You not consider it?"

Sita immediately rectified Her logic and said, "When you carry Me on your shoulders and leave Lanka, the entire *rakshasa* army will attack you from all directions. In the process of fighting them, you may forget about Me, and I could fall into the ocean and drown. That's why I don't want to come with you."

Hanuman couldn't help but laugh again. Even this reasoning did not fit in with Sita's personality. "O Mother, You are Bhumisuta. The earth is Your mother. Why would You fear the ocean, which is a beautiful way of becoming a part of Mother Earth? This definitely cannot be the real reason You don't want to come."[24]

Realizing that Hanuman was quite clever, Sita found another

---

[23] Respect is born in the womb of humility.

Hanuman genuinely felt that everyone else was better than he was and hence respected every one of his colleagues due to his genuine humility.

[24] When one gives a reason for not being able to do something, one must give a reason that matches one's standard. The reason for inability must match the standard of one's ability.

reasoning. "The real reason is that you are a *para-purusha*.[25] I do not want to touch you and travel on your back."

Hanuman found this reasoning funny too. "My dear Mother, I am Your son. For a mother, a son is never a *para-purusha*. Please come with me or tell me the real reason behind Your unwillingness to come."

After much cajoling, Sita spoke up. She didn't want to say this out loud for fear of embarrassing Rama. Hanuman was insistent, so She decided to tell him the real reason. "Have you considered what historians will write when the story of Rama will be written if I return with you now? They would say that Sita was brought from Panchavati to Lanka by a demon and brought back from Lanka by a *vanara*. The question on every lip would be: What did Her husband Rama do? I do not want anyone to point any fingers at Rama and criticize Him for not being able to protect Me from Ravana. It would be glorious only if Rama came here, defeated Ravana and took Me back with Him with dignity and grandeur."[26]

Hanuman's eyes welled up with tears when he heard Sita's reason for not wanting to accompany him back to Rama. Hanuman was taken aback by Her willingness to forgo Her safety for Rama's reputation. Realizing that there was no other way except for Rama to come and destroy Ravana, Hanuman readied himself to leave. No more waiting was needed. But before he left, he asked Sita to give him a token that would remind Rama about Her and reconfirm that Hanuman had indeed met Her. Sita smiled and assured him that

[25] A man who is not the husband.

[26] Intense love is unaltered even by inconvenience.

She would give him two tokens that would beyond doubt convince Rama—a verbal memory and a physical token.

The story Sita chose to tell Hanuman was private and personal to Her and Rama. Even Lakshmana was unaware of this incident as it had occurred during an intimate moment between Her and Rama.

"While We were residing in the mountains of Chitrakuta during Our first year of exile, We spent considerable time together in the scenic forests. One day, Rama was lying on My lap and taking a nap. As I was admiring His beautiful sleeping face, a black crow began to attack Me viciously. Not wanting to disturb Rama's slumber, I tried throwing stones and pebbles at the crow to shoo it off. No matter how much I tried, I was unable to chase it away. The crow's attacks had become more and more vicious now. I began to bleed at various places from the crow's pecking. As I turned and swiveled to avoid the attacks, Rama woke up, only to see Me covered in blood. He became wildly angry with the tormentor. Plucking out a single strand of grass from the ground, Rama chanted some mantras converting that simple grass into the most powerful missile in the universe, the *Brahmastra.* Once he threw the missile at the miscreant, it chased him throughout the universe, not giving him any relief from his sufferings. Only when the demon crow or *kakasura* came back and surrendered at the feet of Rama did the missile slow down.

After a lot of pleading and request for pardon, Rama reduced the effect of the *Brahmastra*, and it only took away one eye of the rogue crow. We decided to keep this story Our little secret." Sita concluded. "The moment you mention this story to Rama, He will know that We have Met. As I remember this story of His love for Me and His anger toward those who tormented Me, I wonder why He hasn't come to protect me from Ravana whose torture has been a million times worse than the crow's. If He could send the

Brahmastra across the universe to annihilate that crow, why hasn't He sent even one to annihilate this demon in Lanka?" [27]

Sita began to sob yet again. Hanuman realized that he had to say something to stop Her from crying and give Her hope. "My dear Mother, Your complaint is that Lord Rama has forgotten You, but my observation is that Lord Rama has forgotten His nature. From the time He has lost You, He has forgotten His own powers. He has completely forgotten the power of His bow. You still remember His prowess, but He has forgotten His own capabilities. If only He remembered His own strengths, You would not be here until now. All day long, Lord Rama is immersed in thoughts about You and worries about You."

Hanuman's words felt like a salve on Her wounded heart. She told him, "My dear son, please do not remind Rama about Me now, instead go and remind Him of His powers. Remind Him of the strength of His mighty bow with which He had single handedly destroyed fourteen thousand demons."

Hanuman was happy that his words had the desired effect. Sita continued recollecting Her private moments with Rama. "Once while We were in the forest, Rama noticed that the red vermilion on My forehead was smudged. He called Me to His side and said that He would rectify it and apply it fresh. He picked up a red ore stone He had found in the forest path and made a paste on His palm. He pulled Me toward him and held My face gently with His hand. Not only did He rectify the mark on My forehead, but He also applied the red vermilion paste on My cheeks.

---

[27] Stories are verbal memory tokens that take one into the lanes of memorable loving experiences.

I also recollect something that happened in Ayodhya much before the exile. One evening, I was waiting for Rama in the palace gardens. Although I waited for quite a long time, He didn't turn up as promised. When He arrived, it was too late and I was very angry. When I asked Him the reason for the delay, He said that He was caught up in work. I was so angry that I told Him that He didn't have any work but was late intentionally. I told Him that since He had done something very wrong, He deserved to be punished. I decided to bind Him as a punishment. I picked up a garland made of soft jasmine flowers and tied up His hands. The white garland turned red. I was so surprised to see how delicate Rama was. No one knows about these incidents but Us. When you remind Him of these incidents, He will surely know that You met Me."

As a physical memory to show Rama that Hanuman had actually met Her, Sita took off the tiara on her head and placed it on Hanuman's palms. "As soon as Rama sees the jewel, He will recognize this as My mother's gift to Me on the occasion of Our wedding. I have been wearing this tiara every single day, and it is a symbol of My union with Rama." During the abduction flight, Sita had dropped many of Her jewels to help Rama trace Her, but She had preserved the one dearest to Her. Hanuman carefully held it and inspected it closely. The symbol of Her marriage would now drag Her husband to Her rescue.[28]

Sita then gave a message for Rama through Hanuman. She said, "My dear Lord, I have been in this dangerous and despicable place for the last ten months, moaning constantly because of this separation

---

[28] True love is about defining one's center of gravity. Find out which direction one is gravitating toward during difficult times and one will know one's true love.

from You. I cannot survive this ordeal much longer now. I give You a month to come and fetch Me. If You do not come by the end of the month, I will surely give up My life as I remember You. This is My firm resolve."

one-month deadline

Hanuman panicked! They just had a month now! It took them more than two months to just get here. Here Sita expected him to return to Rama, inform Him, rally the entire army to the south, cross the ocean, wage a war and kill Ravana! All in a span of a month! It seemed impossible. But Hanuman knew there wasn't time to argue about the impracticality of Her suggestion. They had to do their best now.[29]

Hanuman now just wanted to get going. He had to return at the earliest. He offered his respects to Her and assured Her that soon She would see Her beloved and the entire *vanara* horde destroying the kingdom of Lanka. All her sorrows would be eliminated. When Sita realized that Hanuman was preparing to leave, She felt sad. His presence had had such a soothing effect on Her. She requested him to consider staying for another day in some secret place in Ashok *vatika* for more opportunity to bask in his divine company and hear more about Rama. " Your company for these few moments felt like a half-grown crop field receiving rains. I bless You that Rama may always love You."[30]

---

[29] A disturbed mind does not need logic. It only needs hope.

[30] A saint is someone who earns blessings by giving hope.

Hanuman departed after hearing a final reminder from Her about the deadline.[31] Armed with Sita's blessings and a zeal to reunite Her with Rama, Hanuman climbed up the *simpshupa* tree again. He had to carefully plan his next move now. Of course, the next most important thing to do was give Sita's message to Rama to begin immediate action. But right now, a naughty thought played in his mind. That thought only became naughtier as the swinging fruits all around him began to make him feel hypnotized. It was risky. But nothing good was ever achieved without risk. So he jumped…

SITA SETS THE TIMER

The *Ramayana* reaches its climax with this countdown timer that Sita has set. From now on, all events that take place in the *Ramayana* are in a rapid-fire mode keeping in mind the timer set by Sita. Everyone moves in great haste with this deadline in mind. The *Ramayana* moves in such a way that until the last day there is no certainty about anything.

---

[31] With Sita blessing that Rama will always love him, Hanuman becomes very happy knowing that the pressure was off him now. He no longer had to endeavor to get the Lord's love; rather it was Rama's responsibility to love him now.

Chapter 5

Ravaged Garden, Enraged Sovereign

unexpected damage

"Is this a dream? Or a nightmare!" The *Rakshasi* gang had just woken up. They could recognize nothing around them. Some were so confused that they went back to sleep hoping to wake up when things returned to normal.[1]

But the nightmare would linger around no matter how many times they slept and woke up. They realised soon that nothing in Lanka was ever going to be the same again.

The seniors gathered for an emergency meeting to figure out what had happened as they slept. How could their whole world change so suddenly? How could anything go this wrong in the most secure part of Lanka?

[1] People prefer to wrap their minds around ignorance rather than opening the mind to face realities.

While they were immersed in a discussion, they heard a shrill scream from another corner. *Now what?* They stopped talking and stood up to look in the direction of the scream. A plump *rakshasi* was running toward them at unbelievable speed. If it were any other day, they would have had a hearty laugh, but not today. Today was a national emergency. Lanka's most beautiful and favorite garden, the Ashoka *vatika* had been ravaged. Yes, it was totally messed up to the last tree. All upright structures had collapsed; trees were either uprooted or half broken; ponds, bridges, benches, fountains, flowering plants and fruit-bearing trees were all destroyed. The most scenic garden was converted into a cemetery. How could so much happen in a few hours? Why didn't they hear anything while it happened? [2]

Their minds were confused between what had happened and what was happening. This fleeing *rakshasi* was far more audible now. She kept saying something over and over. But it wasn't a word they were familiar with. In fact, many of them had never heard that word being used in Lanka ever.

"Hari! Hari! Hari! Hari!"

What did Hari mean? Why was she insanely repeating it while fleeing? The horror on her face seemed to indicate she had seen a ghost. But why would a *rakshasi* run away from ghosts? They were no less ferocious than ghosts themselves.

The *rakshasi* reached them and fell on her knees. Turning around, she kept saying. "Hari! Hari! Hari…!" with a terrified stare in a particular direction.

---

[2] *Insensitivity is* humor in the wrong environment. It is seeing humor in other's life situations.

Modesty is seeing humor in one's own life situations.

Calming her down, a few others went to find out what had made her scream so much and run in fear. In a few minutes, they all came back screaming, too.

"Hari! Hari! Hari! Hari!"

This time they weren't alone. Chasing them was the hugest *vanara* they had ever seen. A *vanara* so huge that even the tallest of them came up to his knees! The entire gang of *rakshasi*s ran amuck trying to save themselves.

Now it all made sense. Hari was the Sanskrit word for *vanara*. The first *rakshasi* had seen this huge *vanara*, which had made faces at her and scared her. The other *rakshasi*s also met the same fate. What was surprising was that as they were shouting "Hari, Hari, Hari, Hari," which was also the name of Vishnu. The *vanara* seemed to become happier and naughtier![3]

He began to lift huge tree trunks and throw them everywhere. He then suddenly shrunk himself to a very tiny size and ran away.

What was that? The *rakshasi*s were at a loss now. They had no idea who that huge *vanara* was or how he had broken in, despite the highly secure network of Lanka or why he was destroying everything.

It surprised them that although every nook of Ashok *vatika* was

[3] Hanuman was delighted to hear these demoniac atheistic *rakshasi*s in the kingdom of Lanka chanting the name Hari, which is also another name of Vishnu. It gave him great joy, and he harassed them even more to get them to chant more.

destroyed, the section where Sita was seated was unscathed. The *simshupa* tree stood as it was and so did Sita.[4]

Surely, there couldn't be a connection between that giant *vanara* and Sita, could there? "I told you all not to harass her. Now do you believe me? My dream is coming true. Lanka is doomed." Trijata was emphatic.

The *rakshasis* ran to Sita and began badgering Her with questions: "How did all this happen?" "How was the whole grove destroyed in just a few hours?" "How many of them were involved?" "What exactly did you see?" "Did that *vanara* speak to you?" "Some of us thought we had seen you talking to that *vanara*." "Did you talk to him?" "What did you talk to him?" "Do you know him?" "What has he come here for?" "Where did he come from?" "What will he do next?"

Seeing them panic-stricken and all shaken up, Sita tried hard to conceal Her smile. With a straight face, She told them that She had no idea who that *vanara* was. In fact, She confided to them that She was so scared after seeing His size and gigantic form that She felt it was one of the *rakshasas* or Ravana himself in disguise. She told them that though the *vanara* came very close to Her and tried to talk to Her, She was too scared to even open Her mouth.[5]

---

[4] Exceptions always demand inspection.

[5] Karma is like a boomerang: what one throws at others boomerangs right back.

The rakshasis troubled Sita so much, now they were being troubled.

Sita's Lie

Why Sita lied when questioned by the *rakshasis* is debatable. Was it right for Sita, a follower of dharmic principles, to lie? The Vedic principles allow one to lie during five situations of life.

1. To save one's marriage – *vivaahakaale*.
2. Amid courtships – lovers are allowed lies that enhance love for one another – *rathisamprayoge*.
3. To save one's life from some danger – *praanaathyayae*.
4. To save one's wealth from being stolen – *sarvadhanaapahaare*.
5. To protect a friend in danger – *mithrasya cha arthe*.

To protect the life of Hanuman, She hid his connection with Her. If Ravana came to know that Hanuman had come for Her, his fury would escalate. Thus, considering what was beneficial for Hanuman, She lied.

On getting no answers from Sita whatsoever, the *rakshasis* went around Ashok *vatika* carefully inspecting the damage. As they walked all around the outer wall of the garden, they saw the security guards lying dead, smashed in various inhuman ways. From the way they lay, the *rakshasis* deduced that the poor guys had no clue what hit them and had no chance to retaliate. Once the security guards were knocked out, creating havoc in the garden became easy. But that still didn't explain how none of them heard any noise of the destruction. Either they were too drunk or that the *vanara* had some mystical power to keep them unconscious. What really mattered now was how to deliver the bad news to Ravana and how to stop the still ravaging villain? Of the two, the second one was clearly out of their scope of action. As the *rakshasi* gang ran out of the Ashoka *vatika* toward Ravana's palace, Sita smiled. Good days had finally arrived.[6]

information explosion

Ravana was immersed in a high-level meeting with his most important ministers. His wrangle with Sita wasn't the best way to begin his day. He wasn't over the harsh words spoken by Her. They pierced his ears like a bunch of thorns together. He had plunged himself into the state affairs from the moment he returned so that his mind would have no time to dwell on the insults She had heaped upon him.[7]

Suddenly, a loud commotion filled the court hall and hundreds of *rakshasis* rushed in a state of panic. This had never happened in the history of Lanka. No one had dared enter the courtroom without prior approval or invitation. Some people were never allowed to enter the courtroom. These *rakshasis* were in that category and were not permitted entry anywhere other than the Ashoka *vatika* premises. Ravana was disgusted by this ill-mannered entry. They had broken all etiquette of the courtroom. Controlling his anger,

---

[6] Good luck depends on the crutches of friendship to walk into one's life. Hanuman carried good luck into Sita's life.

[7] A mind filled with fault focuses on losses.
A mind filled with gratefulness focuses on blessings.
Harsh words may be spoken once but they echo eternally.

Ravana decided to hear them out. This had better be something serious else he was going to take them to task.[8]

When everyone began speaking simultaneously, Ravana flung his wine goblet toward them to silence them. He needed calmness when understanding a problem. Turning toward Trijata and Surpanakha, his trusted people in that gang, he raised his eyebrow.[9]

Trijata began speaking. "We bear bad news for you, O King. Your favorite garden, the Ashoka *vatika*, is destroyed. A lone giant *vanara* wreaked havoc in your gardens. We have no idea how this single *vanara* accomplished this task so discreetly. He is powerful and fearless. Just looking at him sent shivers down our spine."

For the first time ever, Ravana burst into tears. No one in Lanka had ever seen a weak moment in his life. He was always this larger-than-life brave king to them. The *rakshasis* were shocked to see him break down at the news about his favorite gardens. But they also knew that once his mood changed, they were in for big trouble.[10]

"What about Sita? Is she safe?" That was his only concern at this point. If there was anything more important to him than Ashoka *vatika*, it was Sita. The *rakshasis* reported that, surprisingly, the only place in the entire area unscathed was where Sita resided.

---

[8] Every bad action involves some deliberation. While ordinary people find fault in the action, leaders focus on analyzing the deliberation behind the action.

[9] In order to digest food, one needs to eat peacefully. Similarly, in order to understand a problem, one needs to think peacefully.

[10] There is nothing like good and bad news. There is only good and bad perception.

It had remained exactly as it was. But the rest had now become Shoka *vatika*. They informed him that they couldn't understand if the *vanara* left that area unharmed out of respect for Sita or out of exhaustion after destroying everything else. Of course, they also added that it wasn't possible for such a powerfully built *vanara* to be so easily exhausted. One of them felt that the *vanara* had a long conversation with Sita although none of them could vouch for it, as they were too drunk to know the difference between reality and dreams.[11]

As Ravana's sadness waned, his fury began to mount. He was getting angrier by the second as they were filling him with more details. He didn't even want to ask them how they had been sleeping while the *vanara* was destroying everything. He had lost all faith in them. He had to deal with this crisis himself. In his style. He flared up like a funeral fire sprinkled with oil. Tears dripped from his face like oil from a lamp. His anger was inflamed now…[12]

a pain for a gain

Hanuman knew he had hit Ravana where it would hurt him most. He could almost hear the demon king scream in pain… As he waited patiently for an eruption from inside the palace, he contemplated his next move.[13]

---

[11] The common person lives reality.
The leader lives dreams.
The drunk is lost between reality and dreams.

[12] Anger is a gift others give for their mistakes.

[13] When one decides to stamp on a dog's tail, one can't prepare for a friendly lick.

He remembered Jatayu. He had not only informed Rama about Sita's abduction, but he had also put up a tough fight against Ravana.[14]

He decided to first teach the demons a lesson on Rama's strength, then study their strengths and weaknesses in war carefully, and finally have a rendezvous with Ravana and destroy his peace of mind.

He had not used any of the four enemy-dealing techniques when trying to find Sita, knowing that those were useless against the demons when he was trying to be discreet. But now that he had already met Her, conveyed Rama's message to Her and heard Her out. Now that there was nothing to hide, he knew the best strategy against the enemy was *danda* or punishment. It made perfect sense to teach them a fitting lesson in a language they understood best – the language of power. Hanuman smiled at his handiwork. The destruction he had caused was ravaging. There was smoke from smashed boulders everywhere, and everything was razed to the ground. Among the ruins, in the lakes, against the rocks and on the trees lay dead and mangled *rakshasa*s. This was the flashiest and most beautiful part of the city, and now it had all turned to dust in a flash.

Hanuman was certain Ravana's rapidly puncturing pride would soon force him to reveal himself. His smile was the widest it had

---

[14] A reliable worker does what is expected.

A reliable leader not only exceeds expectations but surprises others with secondary accomplishments while perfectly executing the primary task. Similarly, a good servant not only accomplishes the primary task he was sent for but also performs a few additional secondary tasks that do not obstruct or impair the original task.

been since he landed in Lanka. He was convinced this quantum of destruction was enough to gain him direct access to Ravana. Although a little voice in his head told him a fraction of this would have been more than enough, he knew his plan had to be foolproof.[15]

He began munching on a fruit as he waited by the arched doorway to Ashok *vatika* for Ravana's pain to explode.

seeds of destruction

When they entered the garden, dust fumes were everywhere. Everything was in ruins. The famed royal gardens of Lanka, the pride of their king, seemed like a crematorium now. The only tree still standing was the *simshupa* tree under which Sita was seated. They searched carefully, but the destroyer was nowhere to be seen. The forces fanned out in every direction to comb him out. Assuming the culprit was hiding in fear, they approached Sita's tree. The only person alive there was Sita. The rest were either dead or had fled. With clubs and iron mallets in their hands, deformed and pot-bellied tusker *rakshasa*s searched for the mischief maker.

As soon as the leader of the eighty thousand Kinkara men Ravana had deputed to investigate the Ashoka *vatika* crisis approached Sita, he heard a crunching noise from among the foliage of the tree. He went closer only to have a half-eaten apple smashed into his face. Stunned and humiliated, he ordered one of his men to climb the tree to force out the hidden animal. As soon as the man reached the top, he felt a hard kick on his ribs that sent him flying off the branch straight to his death.

---

[15] Destruction may destroy everything, but it creates one thing: attention.

Alerted by the moans of the dying man, the army huddled to counter their hidden enemy. Hanuman stepped out from behind the leaves and stood on a thick branch, with one hand on his hip and the other holding a branch. His strong physique intimated the soldiers. As they let out a collective gasp, Hanuman lunged forward, and on his way down kicked two soldiers on their heads, crushing their skulls and killing them instantly. The leader gulped, mustered courage and ordered his men to attack.

Thousands of soldiers rushed toward Hanuman with raised weapons like moths rushing toward a blazing fire. They hurled their weapons at him from all directions. Hanuman merely smiled at the onslaught of thousands of maces, mallets and arrows. "Jai Sri Rama!" Hanuman's war cry was nothing like they had heard before. Before they could even begin to understand it, they heard a whack and a swish and witnessed the instant and simultaneous thwarting of their weapons. All of them lay wasted on the ground. It had all happened so fast that they could not see Hanuman's tail swing across to render the weapons inactive.[16]

They had never seen anything like that since becoming warriors. Before they could gather their wits, they saw Hanuman run toward a damaged archway and pick up a broken iron bar. He began to swing it wildly, sending them back flying but with severed limbs. Every time he hit any of them, he would shout out the same thing: "Jai Sri Rama!" In a flash, all the eighty thousand men were martyred, and Hanuman was back munching fruit until the next batch of soldiers arrived.

---

[16] Hanuman perfected the art of using every limb of his body including his tail for the service of God and humanity.

giant slayer

A lake of liquor. That is what it was. And floating in it was Jambumali, the mighty son of the Lankan minister Prahasta. The Lankan soldiers had reached there to request him to challenge or even defeat what they had understood as a formidable enemy. Their hopes seemed to drown in the intoxicants their leader was soaking and slumbering in. Quite oblivious of their arrival, the star warrior continued with his liquor binge. He would wake up, dip his goblet into the lake, fill it up with liquor, gulp it down and soak in the heady liquid again. He so loved his drink that he'd rather stay immersed in it than have someone bring his drink to him. Of all the drunks they had seen in Lanka, Jambumali had the top honors. Apparently, Ravana had created this liquor lake for Jambumali because of his love for liquor and his extreme restlessness. The demon was fine for as long as he stayed inebriated, but the moment he woke up or stepped out of the lake, he was uncontrollable. He had this unstoppable urge to attack all the time. He was in a permanent state of war and massacre when not soaking in liquor, so much so that he didn't care if he was killing his own people. Ravana could not afford dead soldiers in his own land.[17]

The soldiers realized that Lanka was in a state of emergency and that they had to fetch their star soldier to address the situation. One of the soldiers jumped into the lake and swam up to the floating demon and quietly slipped anti-liquor medicine into his goblet and returned ashore. They waited patiently for him to sit up for another swig of liquor. He woke up sooner than they had expected and unwittingly

---

[17] While most people do good to the world when awake, some contribute best when asleep.

downed the antidote instead. Within seconds, it worked its magic and they could see Jambumali's insides revolting enough to wake him up from intoxicated slumber. The giant demon began to thrash around violently, realizing that he had been tricked. He swam to the shore to unleash his rage on the troops.[18]

They were afraid but had been anticipating this. So before he could start turning them to pulp, they knew what they had to say. One of them said the words, "the king is anxious" and started to brief him about the emergency as fast as he could. These words halted Jambumali. He realized that the situation was graver than he had imagined, so he rushed to Ravana's courtroom to answer the call of duty.

Even though he knew all was not well, the arrogant Jambumali always put his pleasure first. "Why have you brought me down from paradise? It had better be for a good reason." Ravana despised that tone, but at this moment he had no option but to grit his teeth and get on with it. Jambumali was one of his powerful weapons. He knew that when nothing and no one else worked, He could turn to Jambumali. This was one such occasion.[19]

"There is a tough fight waiting for you!" Ravana said.

Nothing excited Jambumali more than a good fight. He felt he was born for such occasions. "Whom do you want me to fight this time? Indra or Agni?"

---

[18] Rather than being angry with those who wake one to the realities of life, one should be angry with those who make one snuggle in ignorance.

[19] Tolerating a dish that tastes bad is easy when accompanied by other tasty items. Similarly, tolerating imperfection in a person is easy if accompanied by some benefits.

"A *vanara*!" Ravana said. Jambumali did notice the tinge of concern in his king's voice, but dismissed it.

"What nonsense! I am going back to sleep. Send one of your tiny soldiers to deal with the *vanara* nuisance." Jambumali thought it was beneath his skills to spar with a *vanara*.[20]

"Ashok *vatika* has been destroyed." Ravana's anguish over the demolition of his favorite and most secure garden was quite evident. "He is no ordinary *vanara*. He has already killed hundreds of our soldiers. He needs to be stopped now."

Even Jambumali's hungover brain knew this trouble had to be managed. He agreed to take on this assignment. In his head, however, he thought this was too small a threat to pull him out of his liquor sauna. Ravana sent along eighty thousand soldiers to assist him. It was below Jambumali's dignity to take help, but he relented on Ravana's insistence.[21]

When the soldiers reached the borders of Ashok *vatika*, they saw a gigantic monkey gobbling a fruit atop the highest dome of a palace.

As soon as he saw the army, Hanuman stood up and placed his hands on his hips and said. "Who wants to die today? I am the servant of Lord Rama. Who has the guts to challenge me?"

Jambumali looked like a powerhouse in his solid armor, crimson garland, maroon silken garments, shimmering earrings and a huge

---

[20] People who wait for a big fight to prove themselves don't realize that life is a series of little fights.

[21] Those who seek help are not small, and those who offer help are not big.

golden bow. Everytime he passed by, the sight of his colossal body would send tremors through the hearts of his enemies. He arrived on a chariot yoked to giant donkeys. Jambumali yelled out a challenge. "You foolish *vanara*! Don't you know where you are standing? You are in the abode of the mighty Ravana. The demigods are chopping vegetables in the kitchen. The *nava grahas*[22] that decide ordinary people's destinies are now fated to serve Ravana as footholds to his throne. My father Prahasta eats giant mountains and digests them like peanuts. I am Jambumali, the harbinger of your death."[23]

Hanuman took his words very lightly. "All that was in the past. The present is *me*. Look at the state of Lanka. I have destroyed all your beautiful gardens."[24]

Jambumali was so furious with Hanuman's retort that he began shooting arrows at him. Hanuman jumped off the dome and landed next to a tree, uprooted it and hurled it at the demon. Soon, a volley of rocks and trees followed. Jambumali shot down the rustic weapons with his arrows and began to send deadly missiles to down Hanuman. Hanuman laughed at his useless shower of weapons as he grabbed and flung those back at the army. A few of Jambumali's arrows did inflict some gashes on Hanuman's body and face, but the blood from these only enhanced his beauty and didn't disturb him at all.[25]

---

[22] Nine planets.

[23] Wherever there is a claim for immortality, there is also great fear of death.

[24] Those who live in the past are often blind to the present realities. Abstain from talking tall about the past in the present drama of life.

[25] When people with strong character bleed, their integrity doesn't flow away but their inner substance shines forth.

Jambumali soon realized that his weapons would be futile against Hanuman, so he decided to resort to magic. He closed his eyes and began to expand himself. He grew until Hanuman was only as high as his knees. With renewed confidence that he could now crush the *vanara*, Jambumali opened his eyes. All he could see were two round walls right in front of his eyes. *What are these?* He began to look all around to understand these objects he had never seen before. Suddenly, he heard a booming voice from high above him. He strained his neck to look up. Hanuman was staring down at him. The round objects he saw were Hanuman's knees. He had expanded to his maximum, but Hanuman had grown much bigger than he could have imagined. Jambumali realized that he couldn't grow any larger now.[26]

When he understood that his individual power wasn't enough to counter Hanuman, he decided to use the entire might of the eighty thousand soldiers. He looked back to direct his army, but in its place saw a huge mountain. *Where was the army?* It didn't take Jambumali too long to understand that while his eyes were closed during his expansion, Hanuman had not only grown to a much larger size but had also lifted an entire mountain and crushed all the soldiers under it. It had all happened in the blink of an eye, and neither Jambumali nor his army had any opportunity to react.

Hanuman spoke from a position of power and advantage. "My dear Jambu, what will you do now? Will you take refuge at my feet?"

"All of this is an illusion! If you have the courage, return to your original form and face me. I shall also assume my original size."

---

[26] Winning wars is about breaking confidence.
Winning hearts is about building trust.

Jambumali challenged Hanuman.

Both returned to their regular sizes and faced each other. Hanuman began to walk around Jambumali, who had to keep whirling around to face him. He said, "Jambu, these are the last three minutes of your life. I have a suggestion for you. I can teach you a special mantra; it is very small and easy and has only two syllables. It will undo all your sins and more. Not only that, if you chant this mantra while dying, you will reach the highest destination possible. Chant after me. Ra-ma. Ra-ma."[27]

Jambumali was quite surprised at the turn of events. He said, "What nonsense? I have not come to learn mantras from a *vanara*! I have come to kill you."

Hanuman smiled. "Since you cannot really do that, you might as well learn this mantra."

Hanuman's nonchalance was too much for Jambumali's ego. No one had ever taken him so lightly. He rushed toward Hanuman and jumped on to him. Hanuman dug his index finger into Jambumali's navel and lifted him all the way up, above his head and spun him around on his finger. After spinning him at high speed, Hanuman flung him aside. Jambumali lay there lifeless, his innards goaded out of his mouth.

'R..A..M..A! R..A..M..A! R..A..M..A!' Hanuman walked away chanting.

---

[27] The highest form of compassion is kindness shown to a person one hates.

one warrior equals a million

Seven armies moved in on him from seven different directions. Each headed by a son of seven of Ravana's ministers. Each was lustrous like fire. Wielding powerful bows, these exemplary archers edged closer to the enemy. Their immense power was evident from their rippling muscles tearing through their tightly fastened armors. Their chariots rumbled like fast-approaching rain clouds. Flags and banners boasted of their numerous victories. Their gem-studded golden bows appeared like racing rainbows and the arrows like thunderbolts.

Hanuman wasn't even moving or attempting to evade the arrows. He smiled at them. The war-trained youngsters were surprised to see an enemy with such a casual approach. Just to confuse their enemy and force him to react, the seven heroes started crisscrossing each other's paths. Moving at great speeds and simultaneously shooting arrows, they expected to irritate their enemy. At one point, so many arrows were shot at Hanuman that he became as invisible as a mountain concealed by heavy rain showers.[28]

Suddenly Hanuman jumped. He took off toward the sky like a rocket. As he shot upward, the mesh of arrows smashed into smithereens. While airborne, Hanuman started his attack on the seven armies. He punched, struck, kicked, boxed, bit, scratched and roared. Some of the soldiers dropped their weapons and fled upon hearing the *vanara*'s terrifying roars. In no time, the armies fell like a pack of cards. Those that did survive the multidirectional

---

[28] The art of irritating begins with understanding oneself well and then ends up with helping others understand themselves.

assault escaped to save their lives. Fear had gripped the ranks. Even the animals in the army were scared. The elephants trumpeted off key, and the horses sat down and refused to budge. Every chariot was dismantled, splinters were everywhere and blood was splashed in all directions.[29]

The painful screams of dying soldiers echoed through the garden. Eventually, Hanuman tore apart the seven sons and dumped their mangled bodies in a chariot and dispatched it to Ravana's palace. Happy with his achievement, Hanuman sat on the steps of the arch gate like an excited kid waiting for more toys to break.

On hearing about the massacre, Ravana realized that the problem was much larger than he had estimated. The next team had to be selected carefully. He handpicked five of the most trusted and formidable leaders in his *rakshasa* army – Virupaksha, Yupaksha, Durdhara, Praghasa and Bhasakarna. Having individually led their armies to many victories, these five were the perfect response to the current calamity. They had proven themselves in the past and would surely show their excellence now when it was most necessary. Warning them to be careful and not to underestimate the enemy as the dead heroes had, Ravana sent them to the warzone. He warned them that he was convinced that this wasn't a mere *vanara* but possibly an extremely evil spirit in *vanara* form. He assumed the insecure and envious Indra had unleashed this evil spirit.

"I have met *vanara*s like Vali and Sugriva in the past, but none seemed to be anywhere close to this particular *vanara* in strength, intellect, power, mental disposition, mysticism and shape-shifting abilities." Ravana alerted the five chiefs.

[29] A person in fear is different from the person itself.

Armed and prepped, the five chiefs left for Ashoka *vatika* on their speedy armored chariots. Hanuman did not even give them a chance to display their archery skills and began to smash their chariots. He hopped from one chariot to another at lightning speed and destroyed all weapons the chiefs carried, including their bows. He landed on Durdhara's chariot with considerable force, crushing it and killing the rider instantly. On seeing their friend killed so mercilessly, Virupaksha and Yupaksha swung into action. But Hanuman picked up a huge fallen *sala* tree and swung it with such force that the two chariots, the masts and the charioteers were all blown off. Not even the remains of Virupaksha and Yupaksha could be traced.

Praghasa and Bhasakarna could not bear the loss and launched a simultaneous attack from two different directions on Hanuman. They chose a direct onslaught. Rushing up to Hanuman with spears in their hands, the two pierced through the *vanara*'s body on either side. Blood gushed out, but rather than being immobilized, Hanuman was incensed. His loud roar startled the warriors into dropping their spears. Hanuman whacked their cheeks simultaneously. The slaps were so intense that the powerful warriors were sent off flying in different directions. By the time they hit the rough walls, they had perished.

Hanuman's anger was now escalating. Blood flowed from the various wounds on his body. The sweat and dust made his body glisten in the sun. He launched an attack on the rest of the *rakshasa* army. Picking up elephants by their legs, Hanuman smashed them against other elephants, killing them all simultaneously. He threw horses on horses and dashed warriors against warriors with the sole intent of finishing them all. The Ashoka grounds were now filled with corpses of all sizes, shapes and species. Broken chariots, weapons and armors were strewn everywhere. Nothing was alive in Ashoka *vatika* save a panting *vanara* hero.

Since no one was left to carry any news to Ravana, Hanuman wanted to take a breather. He hadn't had a single moment's break since taking off from the Mahendra mountain on the other side of the ocean. He hadn't slept, had hardly eaten anything nor found the time to respond to nature's calls. When Hanuman finally decided to relieve himself, he heard a ruffle behind the bushes. He noticed a Lankan soldier had hidden himself to escape the massacre. Hanuman smiled. He wanted to send an important message to Ravana. He had been looking for the right messenger, and here was one. Hanuman delivered the message and asked the horrified messenger to carry it to Ravana.[30]

gladder bladder

"Did I hear you right?" Ravana could not believe that the *vanara* had urinated into this *rakshasa*'s mouth and had asked him to bear this as a message to Ravana. The warrior had been hesitant to speak and kept repeating that the *vanara* had sent a message to the king. When Ravana forced him to deliver the message, he blurted out that the *vanara* had urinated into his mouth. Ravana's stomach churned. He wanted to throw up in disgust and anger. The *vanara* was clever. By urinating into the Lankan soldier's mouth, he had urinated on Lanka. His message was very clear. He cared a damn

[30] When one chooses the right messenger, the messenger becomes the message.

about the Lankan security forces and its army. His message of insult was well conveyed.

Ravana realized that none of his warriors was a good enough match against the unstoppable *vanara*. He realized that it had to be someone from within the family to counter this enemy. He called his family members to war only when he had no option left. If this *vanara* were not stalled soon enough, he would destroy every soldier in Lanka.

This time, Ravana did not want to take the risk of deputing an incompetent leader, so he sent his own son, the heroic Akshay Kumar. His track record was spotless. He had not lost a single battle and was always high on confidence. Although very young, the boy had mastered every weapon and was very skilled. Each time his father called on him, he felt proud and worthy. He wanted to be where his father was some day. He knew the only path to that crown was through war and bloodbath.

When he heard about the havoc created by the lone *vanara*, he readied himself and mounted his flying chariot. This battle wasn't going to be easy. At first look, Hanuman thought Akshay Kumar resembled Ravana. He seemed like a younger version of his father. It was sad that Ravana had resorted to sending his offspring to fight now. On seeing the chariot, Hanuman knew that it was celestial and was the result of many penances and austerities. Protected on all sides with a golden armor and adorned with a flagstaff studded with gems, the chariot was drawn by eight excellent flying horses. The chariot moved like the sun in the vast skyways, effulgent and unrestricted. Moving in circles, Akshay glared at Hanuman with angry yellow eyes. One leap, and Hanuman reached Akshay's chariot and smacked it with his palm. The entire chariot shook dangerously as its wheels and axles came apart. The horses lost control and plunged in different directions. The mast broke into half and dropped on Akshay's head. Finally, the chariot toppled and Akshay began plummeting headlong toward the earth. His weapons fell out of his hands, and he panicked as his descent became faster. Suddenly something broke his fall. He felt his feet being grabbed. The huge *vanara* was holding his feet with just one hand. Suddenly, he had begun to whirl Akshay around. First he was diving down, then he was spinning; he had no control over his body now. Not to prolong matters, Hanuman swirled him around several times before smashing him to the ground. His head was now pulp, and all his bones powder. Akshay, the eternal one, had become *kshay*, the mortal one.

WHAT IS IN A NAME?

Ravana named his son Akshay Kumar, which means the one with immortal youth. Ravana became sad because his son had become Kshay Kumar, meaning the one who died young.

Ravana named his garden as Ashoka *vatika*, meaning the garden of no sorrow. Ravana was upset because his garden had become Shoka *vatika*, meaning the garden of lamentation.

The problem was not in naming, but in the expectation that people and things will live up to the name given.

loss over endless loss

In a matter of few hours, Ravana had lost about two hundred and fifty thousand men at the hands of a single *vanara*. He called an emergency meeting to strategize. First the eighty thousand Kinkaras, then Jambumali with another eighty thousand *rakshasas*, then seven sons of his ministers with their armies, then five most powerful generals of his army and finally his own son Akshay Kumar. The loss was colossal.

Although Ravana was filled with pain and anger at the death of his son, he knew moments such as these required great composure. If Akshay had not lasted a few minutes in front of that *vanara*, no other Lankan hero could. Ravana knew exactly how to tame this *vanara*. But if the king had to go catch a lone *vanara*, it wouldn't reflect well on the state of the armed forces. In fact, that would be a greater insult to the kingdom, which was what the *vanara* seemed to be aiming for. He was trying to destroy the morale of the kingdom with his antics.

The only way according to Ravana was to use celestial missiles. Not all warriors in Lanka possessed celestial weapons. Ravana was adept in the use of every celestial weapon as was his eldest son, Indrajit. He had named him Meghnad first, but he bestowed the name Indrajit on him after his victory against Indra, the king of gods.

Ravana briefed him about the Ashoka *vatika* fiasco and prepared Indrajit's mind for the upcoming war. "Remember about your great victories against the celestials and other powerful forces. Do not use regular weapons in this fight as they would all prove useless. Use selective celestial weapons and capture the *vanara* alive. This mission will test your penances and intellectual astuteness. Be warned that your army will be useless in this combat and don't rely on numbers in this war. This is a fight to be fought with calmness rather than anger. The *vanara* will try his best to agitate you and disturb your cool. If he does that, it's even more critical that you remain calm. Promise to avenge your deceased brother. Now go and be victorious in this critical *vanara* mission." Ravana sent off his son on this crucial mission with his blessings. Indrajit bowed to his father and mounted his chariot, which was drawn by four huge tigers.[31]

The rattling sound of Indrajit's unique chariot and the twanging of his bow was music to Hanuman's ears. He had been waiting for a tougher fight. These *rakshasas* were a disappointing lot that died even before he began fighting. He had heard so much about the Lankan army's heroism and prowess. At this moment, all of that seemed like glib talk. He hoped for a worthier opponent.[32]

As soon as he spotted the rogue *vanara*, Indrajit began spraying arrows at him. Hanuman was so agile and quick that not even one arrow touched him. Being the son of the wind god, Hanuman used wind energy to divert the arrows very subtly to avoid harm. When Indrajit saw Hanuman's ploy, he began to use heavier arrows. Hanuman found other ways to deflect them. After repeated attempts, Indrajit found no weakness in Hanuman. He was agile both physically and mentally.

On realizing that he could not kill or injure the *vanara*, Indrajit thought of an alternate path. He nocked onto his bow a missile

---

[31] Most fights are fought mentally first and physically next.
Leaders win the mental fight before launching into the physical one.

[32] Reality is always more disappointing than one's imagination.

Lord Brahma had given him and murmured a mantra. Hanuman could feel the power of Indrajit's missile as he chanted the mantra. Just by the vibrations in the environment, Hanuman knew this was a Brahma missile. He knew he could not disrespect it.

losing to win

He stood with folded hands and received the missile on his chest. As soon as the arrow hit his body, it transformed into a rope and started binding him tightly. Once the missile tied his legs together, Hanuman lost his balance and fell to the ground. He closed his eyes and expressed his gratitude to Lord Brahma for everything he had done for him in his life. He could feel the protective paternal embrace of the secondary creator around his body. He recollected all the blessings Lord Brahma had given him in his childhood. One of these was that no weapon offered by him would ever bring him harm or affect him. Hanuman knew that Brahma's rope would disentangle whenever he wanted it to. He had done enough damage in Lanka. Ravana's complete attention was on him, and he could effectively communicate his message now. Ravana was so filled with arrogance that only a damage of this magnitude could draw his attention.

When the *rakshasas* saw a fallen Hanuman, there was uproar in the army ranks. Many of the *rakshasas* rushed toward the fallen *vanara* with more ropes and tree barks to ensure he was securely bound. They were not sure if the Brahma rope hurled by Indrajit was enough to keep the *vanara* under control. If by chance there were an error, the agile *vanara* would slip off and resume his destructive spree.[33]

---

[33] The higher the stake, the higher is the fear of the consequence of making

When Indrajit saw his *rakshasa* army being overenthusiastic about tying up the *vanara* with more ropes, he could only knock his own head at their ignorance. If only they would stop to understand that once more methods of binding were used on someone already bound by the Brahma missile, its effect was sure to wear off. The Brahma bondage could not coexist with a bondage of another kind. Indrajit was, however, hopeful that the *vanara* was just as ignorant about it as these *rakshasas*.[34]

The *rakshasas* began to drag the bound Hanuman toward Ravana's palace. Beating the intruder with sticks and clubs, the cruel *rakshasas* jeered at him. Although heaped with insults and abuses, Hanuman grinned. He knew his turn would come soon. He noted the faces of those that troubled him the most. He had special plans for them. As Indrajit walked alongside the *rakshasas* dragging the imprisoned *vanara*, he noticed that sarcastic grin. He wondered what it meant. *Why is he grinning? Were they taking him, or did he want to be taken? Were they playing with him, or was he playing with them? Was he in trouble, or were they in trouble?*

---

a mistake.

One must find one's stake before judging one's mistake.

[34] One must not include other's inabilities in being lenient with one's mistakes.

Chapter 6

The Formidable Foe

the dashing demon king

aho roopam aho dhairyam
aho satvam aho dyutihi
aho rakshasa raajasya
sarva lakshana yuktataa

"What an impressive form! What magnificence! What valor! What potency! This great personality, the king of the *rakshasa* world is a blend of all propitious qualities!"

Every time Hanuman saw this demon, the exact same sentiments crossed his mind. Ravana was the most charismatic person he had ever seen in his life. He knew how to carry himself and had an awe-inspiring persona. Ravana spread himself across a large throne made of crystals, embedded with the precious jewels and luxuriously embroidered. He looked splendorous. A precious golden diadem with shimmering diamonds decorated his lustrous face. It was hard to tell if his handsomeness enhanced the crown or the crown's opulence revitalized his face.[1]

Gold and pearl ornaments inlaid with priceless gems adorned his broad chest. The glistening pearl necklace contrasted so gorgeously with his shiny dark body like the lustrous moon against a pitch black night. The king had refined taste even in clothing. His clothes were made of the costliest of silks, his body was smeared with the most fragrant and exotic of red-sandalwood pastes, his limbs had thick golden armlets, bracelets and anklets, and his arms and face had the brightest and the most colorful of artwork. Every single color enhanced the emotions reflected off his facial muscles. His sharp kohl-lined eyes looked luminous and his lips moved to utter carefully chosen words that went straight to the heart. His mouth resembled a snake hole in which his huge tongue slithered like a venomous snake.

Beautiful young girls flanked him as they fanned him with feather *punkahs*. Some of his most important ministers, including Prahasta, Mahaparshva and Nikumbha, were seated right next to his throne on a level lower, always eager to share their wise counsel with him. With them around him, Ravana, the supremo of Lanka, looked like the earth encircled by the four oceans.

Hanuman was impressed. This was the third time he had seen Ravana since landing in Lanka the previous night. His impression of this person's grandeur only increased each time he saw him. He

---

[1] While one should focus on looking good inside, one tends to focus on looking good outside.

While one wants others to focus on one's good-looking outsides, people tend to peep into the insides and discover the ugly bits.

was being dragged into the courtroom toward the central throne but Ravana's splendor seemed to have occupied Hanuman's thoughts.[2]

As Indrajit pulled the rope that was spun around Hanuman, scores of *rakshasa* soldiers surrounded him. As pride shone on every face, doubt clouded Indrajit's. Ravana, on the other hand, was flush with anger on coming face to face with the rogue *vanara* for the first time. The angrier Ravana became, the more his face contorted. His fists kept wringing the armrests of his crystal throne. Hanuman then noticed more heads popping out from the sides of Ravana's face – more fury, more heads. Soon Ravana's broad shoulder had ten identical heads. Bloodshot bulging eyes glimmered with rage on each head, and all those twenty eyes were glaring at Hanuman. Almost as if wanting to turn the *vanara* pest into ashes with his flaming stare. As Ravana's anger mounted, provoked by Hanuman's irreverence, extra arms began to emerge from the demon king's thick shoulders. Before long, twenty powerful fidgety arms flanked his sides. The arms were flaying in every direction, smashing things and throwing goblets of wine all over. As Ravana's rage spread, Hanuman surveyed the majestic room.[3]

Although Hanuman's eyes reflected admiration for Ravana's majesty, they showed a tinge of sadness, too. Here was a magnificent being of superlative intelligence and immense power. If only he were righteous, he could have ruled all the three worlds together with

---

[2] To appreciate a streak of greatness without insecurity is itself a streak of greatness.

Hanuman was not jealous or insecure to be able to appreciate the greatness in Ravana.

[3] Although ice is very cool, it generates great heat. The coolness of some people generates heat in others.

Indra. His unrighteous streak had diluted all his virtues. It was like a droplet of poison in a pot of milk. The act of aspiring for another's wife had made all his superlative assets useless and vicious. If only Ravana had not performed that heinous act, he would have had no match in this world.[4]

As Hanuman admired him, Ravana was assessing Hanuman. *Who is this powerful* vanara? *He isn't any ordinary* vanara *or even a* vanara *warrior. I have seen all of them and have a fair idea of their strengths. But this* vanara *has defied the ordinary. This lone unarmed* vanara *has wiped out one-third of my army.*

The information on the loss had preceded Hanuman's arrival. So Ravana knew that an unbelievable number of his soldiers had perished without even the formal declaration of war. *How is he so powerful? Where is he from? What is his purpose in vandalizing Lanka?* Ravana was looking for answers to these burning questions by studying the intruder's face and body language. But there was no clue there.[5]

Ravana began to revisit his memory palaces to find something in his past. Perhaps someone he had mistreated had come back for revenge

---

[4] Just as one drop of poison can destroy the effects of a million drops of nectar, one poisonous vice can dilute the effect of a million virtues.

[5] Some commentaries say that Ravana admired Hanuman for his great vigor and asked him the source of his strength. Hanuman replied, "The same as yours." Hanuman did his best to make Ravana realize that there was a greater power than him: Lord Rama, the source of all powers. But Ravana did not budge from his ignorance. This exasperated Hanuman who condemned himself for Ravana's misplaced admiration in him instead of Lord Rama.

or some sage had created a monster to destroy him.[6] As he struggled to navigate his memory lanes, he recollected a curse hurled at him by Nandi, the bull carrier of Lord Shiva. When he was on his first ride on the *pushpak vimana*, he had accidentally entered the private section of Lord Shiva on Kailash and had been stopped by Nandi. Ravana had laughed out loud on seeing Nandi's face. As he burst out laughing, mocking Nandi and calling him *vanara*-faced, Nandi had said, "I curse you that *vanaras* will soon destroy your country." *Is this Nandi's curse in action? Is this* vanara *Nandi himself disguised to fulfill his own prophecy? Or is this Banasura, the son of King Bali from the Patala provinces?* Not wanting to lower his dignity by talking to a lowly *vanara*, Ravana ordered the trusted Prahasta to conduct the inquiry. He signaled him to eke every detail out of the *vanara* by whatever means possible.[7]

Prahasta spoke as a mediator would, setting aside his personal anger and sadness. This *vanara* had ruthlessly killed his son Jambumali and yet was expected to question the rogue. He was boiling with rage, but he had to appear calm. "O *vanara*, know that you are now a prisoner of Lanka. Whatever you say here in the Lankan court will be either used against or for you. Choose every word carefully because that will decide your fate. If there is any deceit, know that it will lead to your death. No one has ever managed to lie and survive in Lanka. Do not be afraid, and tell us the complete truth. I only want answers to two questions at this point: First, who are you and second, who sent you here? Although you appear to be a *vanara*, you cannot be one, for your strength and splendor far exceed that of any other *vanara*.

---

[6] Most of today's burning questions are the consequence of yesterday's chilling choices.

[7] Fear today is a result of the mistakes of the past one assumed one had gotten away with.

You seem to have come here with a clear purpose. Has King Indra of the heavens sent you here? Has Kubera of the Kailash mountains sent you to spy on Lanka? Has Yama of Naraka, the god of death, appointed you? Has Varuna, the god of the seas, sent you with his waves? Or has Lord Vishnu, the Lord of Vaikuntha, sent you as a messenger? Why did you destroy Ashoka *vatika*? Why did you kill so many *rakshasas*? If you answer these questions truthfully, then we will release you and spare your life. If you speak a single lie, your chance of survival will be bleak."[8]

Without even caring to look at Prahasta, Hanuman spoke looking directly at the king. "Know for sure that I am neither a spy for the celestials nor a messenger of Lord Vishnu. I am an ordinary *vanara* from the *vanara* kingdom of Kishkinda."

> *"Darshane raakshasendrasya*
> *durlabhe tad idam maya*

To meet the king of *rakshasas* is very difficult. I found an easy way to get an appointment with the king by destroying what was dearest to him. And here I am in your presence, O King. I did not plan to destroy your soldiers. That was in self-defense. They had attacked me first."[9]

---

[8] A thief talking about honesty is like ice talking about longevity. Both don't last long.

Managing emotions is like managing colors in a painting. Just as some contrasting colors make the most beautiful combinations, the most contrasting emotions always lurk around together.

Prahasta had to manage his emotions related to his son's death and had to perform his duty of interrogating the killer without agitation.

[9] Destruction sometimes is the best way to gain attention.

the irreverent monkey's warning

Hanuman was indifferent about the entire episode. He was even smiling. "Oh, by the way, there is one thing you need to know. Your soldiers are ignorant. They have no sense and don't even understand weapons or the rules related to those weapons. I surrendered to Brahma's noose that your son threw at me only for a reason – to meet you. Despite me being bound by the noose, your soldiers, who were only too scared, tied me with hundreds of other ropes. It simply nullified the effect of the *Brahma pusha*, and the celestial noose is no longer effective in binding. O King, I have taken all this trouble with the only intent of giving you some good advice that none of your able ministers and family members seem to have given you so far."[10]

The more Hanuman spoke, the more Ravana fumed. Hanuman then made a demand. "O King, I am a guest in your court, don't you know that a guest has to be treated with utmost respect? Now that you know that I am about to give you some good advice, would it not be prudent to offer me a seat?" The whole court gasped. *A prisoner demanding facility from a king!*

With the whole courtroom staring at him with contempt and disgust, Hanuman decided to help himself. The next moment his tail touched the ground and coiled up. Everyone saw it becoming stiff and coiling over and over until a stacked loop was created. When the loops reached his waist, Hanuman sat atop the tail stack. Soon the makeshift seat began to increase in size even faster.

[10] Since good advice is often rejected as bad intention, good advisors become silent spectators.

In a matter of moments, Hanuman was seated on top of a huge seat made of his own tail, a seat that was a few levels higher than Ravaṇa's. Ravana's throne was nine steps above ground level and Hanuman's tail-throne was way above that. Ravana had to look up at the smiling Hanuman.[11]

The courtroom fell silent. No one dared breathe. Repeated insults had been heaped on their king, but he hadn't responded yet. It was obvious their king's fury had peaked. But there was only one thought on everyone's mind. *Why isn't he doing anything yet?* As uncertainty prevailed in the Lankan courtroom, Hanuman continued his extempore speech.

satyam raakshasaraajendra
shrunushva vachanam mama
rama daasasya dhootasya
vaanarasya viseshatah

"Truth I speak, O king! Listen carefully to these words of mine. Know me to be Rama *dasa*, the servant of Rama. Know me to be Rama *doota*, the messenger of Rama. I am simply an ordinary *vanara* on a special mission.

The message I carry is one of righteousness, one of peace, one of *dharma*. The son of Dasaratha, the late king of Ayodhya, was exiled to the forest for fourteen years. While He lived in the forest along with His wife Sita and brother Lakshmana, Sita went missing. During the search, the brothers reached the *vanara* kingdom of Kishkinda and met up with Sugriva. Their identical life

---

[11] Hanuman tried to convey to Ravana that thinking higher was more important than sitting higher.

circumstances brought Rama and Sugriva together. Rama eliminated Vali and enthroned Sugriva as the king of the *Vanara* clan. The grateful Sugriva reciprocated by sending *vanaras* across the world to look for Sita. I am but one of the soldiers on this mega mission. I jumped across the ocean and landed in Lanka and examined every inch of it. During my search, I came across Sita and saw Her held captive in Ashoka *vatika*. O King, you are a wise man. You know the codes of *dharma* very well. Isn't it against those codes to hold captive another's wife? I must caution you that if you want a life of peace and joy, you must return Sita immediately. Rama will forgive any lapses on your part.

If you are under any illusions that Sita is under your custody, then I must tell you only a foolhardy person can assume that fire can be held in a cloth. Even gods and demons with their combined forces cannot hold Her captive with their prowess. Even with the strongest power of digestion, none can survive after consuming poison. This one act of yours will ruin all the merits that you have gained over lifetimes of penance and hard work. The only reason you live such a life of luxury is because of all the *tapasya*, austerities and sacrifices you have undertaken. But this act of yours is enough to destroy all that piety, just as a single arrow from Rama's bow is enough to destroy the most powerful Vali, whose strength you know.[12]

Adharma can never suppress *dharma* for too long. Soon *dharma* will triumph. Rama has vowed to destroy the abductor of His wife. Rama's vow and bow both never fail. All the other women that you have troubled in the past may not have caused you much harm, but Sita is fire. She is like the night that envelopes the sky and like

---

[12] There seems to be only a one-letter difference between the words *film* and *life*. Yet the key difference is that in life there are no retakes for mistakes.

Yama's death noose. She will consume Lanka with Her purity and reduce it to ashes. Do not invite the destruction of your race. Just as you lost one son today, you will lose all your sons, relatives, friends, counselors, ministers and well-wishers. Rama destroyed fourteen thousand soldiers of Khara and Dhushan single-handedly. On the other hand, I have seen you tossed around all over by the tail of an ordinary *vanara* like Vali, whom Rama had killed effortlessly. That Vali has gone and so has his tail.[13]

If Rama decides to eliminate anyone, even Lord Brahma, Lord Shiva and Indra cannot protect that person. The only hope for a person whom Rama is furious with is Mother Sita. For someone facing the wrath of both Sita and Rama there is neither scope to escape nor hope in the three worlds. So, the only option for you, O *Rakshasa* king, is to return Sita to Rama with dignity and seek forgiveness before Rama releases His unstoppable arrow."[14]

Every brow in that room was dripping with sweat. The atmosphere was tense. The *vanara*'s warning boomed across the courtroom loud and clear. Beyond the message, one thing was clear to everyone in that courtroom: the big-mouthed *vanara* was in big trouble!

CLANGGGGGGG!

---

[13] Arrogant people are humble only in the presence of fear; therefore, Hanuman took the name of Vali as he was the only person Ravana feared.

[14] Hanuman was amazed by what the servant Lankini understood in one punch that the master Ravana was unable to comprehend despite so many punches on his ego and extensive direct advice. What did Hanuman want Ravana to realize? That this couldn't be an ordinary monkey's punch. Behind him was the power of Rama.

to kill or not to kill

The loud crashing of the liquor jar on the marble floor shattered the momentary silence that filled the room after the *vanara* had stopped speaking. The king was furious! He started throwing everything he could lay his twenty hands on. Ravana could no longer bear the humiliation a mere *vanara* was subjecting him to.

"Kill him! Kill the arrogant fool!"

Ravana's baritone rang through the entire palace. Wringing his hands and punching his fists on his palms, Ravana paced in front of his throne. He so wanted to run down the steps and slaughter the *vanara* himself. But it was a full courthouse, and he had to control himself. He knew no able king would lose control in such provocative situations. He wanted to follow the court protocol. Soldiers rushed in from all directions to execute the king's instructions. Hanuman jumped off his seat. He was done speaking and was now ready for whatever reaction came his way. As soon as he jumped off, his tail began to shrink and soon was its regular size.

"Wait! We can't do this to a messenger!" An authoritative voice stopped the advancing soldiers in their tracks. All eyes turned to the direction of the voice. It was Vibhishan, Ravana's younger brother. "O King, please forgive my audacity in voicing my thoughts. But considering the greater good of the kingdom and your reputation as king, it's important that I speak up now. My respected brother, you need to be a little patient and more merciful. Wise kings should be careful when dealing with ambassadors. Ambassadors are expected to be provoctive, and they cannot be penalized with a death sentence for it, according to the prescribed codes of statesmanship. Of course, a scholar like you knows the codes of *dharma* well. Please do not decide on an impulse. Do analyze the consequences of your verdict. I agree that this messenger has caused great damage to Lanka. I know he has killed thousands of our soldiers, the sons of our ministers and even our own son, Akshay. He deserves punishment for his misdeeds, but our tradition forbids the killing of an ambassador no matter how vicious his act. If you so wish, you may punish him in any other way you feel appropriate. You may mutilate him, beat him up, disfigure him, whip him, humiliate him, shave him but never kill him.

This ambassador is simply a mouthpiece. He has no will of his own. There is no point in punishing someone relaying a message. How will the killing of this messenger benefit us? If at all we need to kill someone, it should be the person behind the message and not the one delivering it. If we allow this messenger to return, our real enemies will come with their armies. O King, you are the greatest warrior alive, and you love to fight. If Rama and Sugriva come here with the *vanara* army, you can finish them all and emerge victorious. You will then get an opportunity to exhibit your real strength to the world by terminating your enemies all at once. Let the world know honorably that you are the greatest warrior that ever walked the earth. Please understand that the method I suggest is not only honorable but will also help increase your glory as a king."

"Hmmmmmm!" The words of his brother set Ravana thinking. After a minute of deep thought, he came up with an idea to pacify his heart and take care of the rogue *vanara*'s arrogance. "To shatter the pride of a person, it's pertinent to hit where it hurts most. Every person considers something as prized and precious. For a *vanara*, nothing is as dear as his tail. Let us burn this *vanara*'s ornament, his tail. When he returns with a burned tail, his friends and family members will make fun of him. He will remember us each time he is made fun of his charred tail. Let the *vanara* be carried around the whole of Lanka in a procession with a burning tail. His screams of agony will bring relief to all the citizens of Lanka who have lost their near and dear ones as a result of his misdeeds."

FEEDBACK

Vibhishan teaches one the art of giving feedback to someone senior, elder or superior. This is more applicable when giving feedback to those with bloated egos.

The feedback must be sandwiched between forgiveness and glorification. Right at the onset, Vibhishan asked forgiveness from his elder brother. After seeking forgiveness for the audacity he was about to commit, he gave an honest feedback. Then in the same breath began to glorify Ravana's greatness.

Because the feedback was well cushioned between forgiveness and glorification, Ravana could swallow that feedback pill.

Excited by their king's verdict, some *rakshasa*s ran about collecting cloth to wrap around the tail of the *vanara*. Some ran to fetch oil and other inflammable lubricants to soak the fabric in. Some others focused on wrapping the reams of cloth around the tail. Others doused the cloth with the oils. Just when they had finished wrapping his tail with cloth and dousing it with oil, they noticed a large part of the tail still left uncovered. They busied themselves again to cover up that bit. Yet again, a new section was left bare. This continued until the entire floor of the courtroom was filled with cloth-covered oily tail of the *vanara*. There was no more cloth left in the whole of Lanka. The ministers began offering their own vests to be used as wrap cloth. Even Ravana took off his vest. Eventually, the tail stopped growing, and it was completely wrapped up and dipped in oiled. The *rakshasa* soldiers then dragged the *vanara* with numerous chains that had tied him down. They walked toward the gate of the courtroom. Many followed behind lugging the *vanara*'s long and wagging tail.

UNCLOTHED AND EXPOSED

Ravana was an excellent orator, and he used well-adorned language. In the absence of clothes, ornaments serve no purpose and are often unappealing on a bare body. According to Hanuman, Ravana's ornate language was like that of a bare-bodied person decorated with costly ornaments. Clothes, though cheaper than ornaments, are more essential. Without clothes, ornamentation is crass. Hanuman considered Rama's name as cloth and refined language as the ornamentation. Ravana was using refined language but the cloth of Rama *naam* was absent.

When Ravana announced that *vanaras* loved their tails, Hanuman was smiling because the demon king could not be more wrong. He did not know that Hanuman only loved Rama. Ravana may have had enough cloth to tie his tail but not enough to tie Rama.

The cloth that Ravana used represents the material covering and the oil represents the attractions of this world. Ravana himself represents greed. Ravana is trying to cover Hanuman's love with cloth and coat it with oil. That's like greed trying to cover a devotee's love for God with material covering tinged with attractions and attachments. But since the object of Hanuman's love, which is God, is unlimited, it's impossible to cover it up completely.

Hanuman was furious for being treated, chained and dragged around like an animal. He controlled his anger and grinned back at Ravana before being finally towed out of the courtroom. Indrajit, who had seen that ominous smile, squirmed in his seat. He was uncomfortable with this *vanara*'s confidence then, and he was not comfortable with it now. *What is he up to this time?* Indrajit got up and walked behind the entourage to keep an eye on the dangerous *vanara*, who he was convinced had many more tricks up his sleeve.

Chapter 7

Blazing Tail and Charred Egos

parting lash

The soldiers set fire to the cloth-wrapped tail the moment they stepped out of the courtroom. They dropped the tail and stepped aside. Fire spread rapidly, engulfing the entire length of the well-lubricated cloth wrap. The soldiers who had held the chains tightened their grip on it expecting the *vanara* to start howling and writhing in pain. The flames had consumed the cloth and were now licking Hanuman's tail, but he did not flinch. Instead, he had a strange smile fixed on his face. The soldiers began dragging Hanuman through the streets of Lanka with his tail alight. Kettledrums and conches signaled to the citizens to step out of their homes and watch the spectacle. The rogue *vanara* with his tail on fire was passing by and nothing could be more delightful than watching the enemy burn. Citizens gathered outside their homes to see their king's rightful judgment being executed. Some who had lost their loved ones to the *vanara*'s antics were so angry that they pelted stones at him. Even *rakshasa* children were glaring at him angrily. Abuses and filth were hurled at him along the way to humiliate him.[1]

---

[1] In the absence of humility, humiliation breaks you.

Hanuman was seething and strategizing at the same time. Eventually, the strategizing gave way to the seething. He decided to use this humiliation tour around Lanka as an opportunity to observe the city in daylight. The *rakshasas* had started to inadvertently parade him through the most important and secure places in Lanka. Hanuman's eyes had been capturing every tiny detail of the city that could help them when they returned to lay siege on the country. He marked the houses of prominent ministers and other important members of the royal family, homes of soldiers, barracks, weapons installations, liquor warehouses, horse and elephant stables and warriors' leisure zones. Once he had seen enough, he allowed his anger to take over. [2]

Then suddenly, with a loud roar, Hanuman swung around, throwing off all the *rakshasa* soldiers holding the chains tied to his body. In a moment, the captors were all being flung in different directions and sent crashing against walls. Hanuman's throw was so powerful that when the soldiers crashed on the walls, their crushed skulls and torsos splattered blood everywhere. A growing Hanuman broke all his shackles and stomped his feet on the ground causing tremors. Citizens panicked and rushed out to save themselves. *Rakshasa* children began to cry and run to their mothers. Soldiers readied themselves for a fight, their weapons in active mode.

The burning tail had begun to swing around menacingly, forcing everyone to step back to avoid being engulfed by the fire. Now it was Hanuman's turn to have some real fun. He began to prance around,

---

[2] Conscious anger keeps one mentally peaceful while one seems to be physically agitated.

Unconscious anger originates with mental agitation and culminates with physical demonstration.

Hanuman was consciously angry and hence mentally stable even while exhibiting anger.

swishing his tail recklessly. The *rakshasa* men and women now began to panic because of the gravity of the situation. Just few minutes ago, they were having so much fun at this *vanara*'s expense. Now the *vanara* was having fun at their expense. He began setting fire to the beards and mustaches of the *rakshasa* men. As the men ran amok screaming, Hanuman laughed and continued to set fire to houses and shops on the street. The moment anyone saw him hop on to a roof, all residents rushed out to save themselves from being reduced to ashes. All the laughing, guffawing and stone pelting gave way to screaming, panic and scampering to find safer havens in a suddenly insecure city. Hanuman made sure to burn down most establishments of Lankan ministers except that of Vibhishan. The only time Hanuman had heard a *rakshasa* utter the word *dharma* was when Vibhishan said it. He was also grateful to him for having supported him in the courtroom when everyone else was out to destroy him. Not that he needed that support, but he appreciated the gesture. He reciprocated by making sure that Vibhishan's palace was left unharmed.

DHARMA IN THE KINGDOM OF ADHARMA

A grateful heart always looks for some reason to be indebted even when surrounded by many reasons to complain.

To see *dharma* where *dharma* exists in abundance is easy.

To see *dharma* where *dharma* hardly exists is tough.

To see *dharma* where *adharma* exists in abundance is almost impossible.

Through Vibhishan, Hanuman could see a tinge of *dharma* in Lanka, a land heaped with *adharma*.

winds of change

Hanuman targeted marketplaces to drag down the Lankan economy through the losses they were about to incur. As Hanuman watched Lanka in flames and people in commotion, he noticed the wind patterns change suddenly. He had been in Lanka for close to twenty-four hours now, and he had been studying the wind. But since he set the kingdom on fire, the wind patterns had changed completely. He observed and realized that forty-nine kinds of winds were blowing in Lanka at the moment. Initially, he could not figure out the sudden change, but when he noticed the effect of the change, he smiled. After all, when the son was engaged in a mission, why wouldn't the father want to assist? He realized that Vayu, his father and the wind god, had directed all his attention to his mission. As soon as Hanuman set fire to something, Vayu ensured the winds fanned the flames. Hanuman was thrilled at the help he was receiving.

Most citizens of Lanka had by now figured out that there was no way to stop the *vanara* or prevent destruction. As wind and fire together wreaked havoc, they realized that all they could do was save their own lives and that of their near and dear ones. A complete evacuation of the city was being organized. When they turned around, they saw the *vanara* with its tail on fire hopping from rooftop to rooftop like a cloud dropping lightning bolts everywhere. Some thought it looked like the destruction dance of Lord Shiva. As the fire raged, following Hanuman across Lanka, the citizens began to jump into lakes, ponds, fountains and other water bodies to save themselves. Soon every single water body in Lanka was filled with people. Once the local water bodies filled up and there was no space for more, people began to rush toward the ocean.[3]

After finding satisfaction in burning the most important residences and markets of the city, he turned his attention to the pride of the city – the golden palace of the king. While the attention of most warriors and ministers was drawn toward saving their own houses and families, Hanuman darted toward his next target. As he began his climb up the peak of the Trikuta mountain where the palace of Ravana stood tall, his tail was blazing. Hanuman reached the summit within moments. From atop the mountain, a flaming Lanka looked spectacular. But for the palace guards this was no wonderous view but a possible threat to the palace of the king. So far, the fire had been far away from the palace, and everything seemed safe.

Suddenly, a ball of raging fire rushed toward them, breaking open the gates. It burned so bright that they couldn't even clearly see what it was. Even before they could regain their senses, an iron rod smashed into their skulls, killing the whole lot of them instantly. Soon Hanuman was on the dome of the palace. In a matter of minutes, the most opulent palace of the country was an inferno. The whole of Lanka could witness it from below. From the safety of the water bodies, the citizens looked up at their inspiration turning to ash. All the gold in the palace began melting down like the draining determination of the *rakshasas* to fight against their lone enemy. The golden bricks, chandeliers, domes, chariots and cutlery melted away and began to flow down like molten rivers. Hanuman broke the Lankan flag on the topmost dome of the palace and jumped off

[3] Vayu helped Hanuman because he was the father. Agni did not burn Hanuman because he was the friend of his father. Agni always needs Vayu's favor to burn effectively. Fire needs to be fanned by encouraging winds, but wind does not need fire to blow. Because Agni always benefitted from Vayu, he had to help him when his son needed help.

the Trikuta mountain peak and landed straight on the ocean shore. He dipped his still burning tail into the ocean, extinguished the fire and jumped back to the Subela mountain, his first stop in Lanka.[4]

He threw down the flag and looked back at the once golden city. He was standing here just a day ago, admiring the splendor of the golden city and today the narrative had changed. He was admiring the speed at which the fire was devouring the city. The golden city was melting right in front of his eyes. A smile emerged on his face.[5]

That smile turned into a frown. *What was happening?* He couldn't believe his eyes. His entire effort would go to waste now. *How could it rain so much and so suddenly?* Only the area of Lanka that was burning down seemed to be the beneficiary of this downpour. *While Vayu and Agni were cooperating so well, why was Indra messing things? Wasn't he aware of Lord Rama's mission? Wasn't he aware of the atrocities of Ravana? Why wasn't he cooperating now?*[6]

---

[4] To burn the pride of another person, one needs to first burn one's own pride.

Ravana was trying to burn Hanuman's pride, but Hanuman realized that Ravana hadn't yet managed to burn his own pride. Therefore, Hanuman took up that role because he had already burned up his pride by Rama's grace.

[5] When Hanuman entered Lanka, he noticed every house had a deity: the human body. Everyone worshipped Sharira *devata*. When the body must be burned eventually, why worship it? He wanted to teach the Lanka*wasis* that no matter how much they worshipped the body, one had to burn it at the end of life. He wanted to bare this truth of life to them by burning Lanka.

[6] The most unreliable friends are those that exhibit non-cooperation in the garb of cooperation.

The most trustworthy friends are those that exhibit cooperation in the garb of non-cooperation.

Just as all these questions plagued Hanuman's mind, Indra appeared before him. Even before Hanuman could launch his verbal attack, Indra said. "Look toward the still-raging fire." Hanuman was surprised to see that the fire was still burning despite the rain. By now the rains had stopped, but instead of dousing the fire, it had rekindled it. The fire now seemed unstoppable, as it had wildly spread to every nook of Lanka. Indra explained, "I have caused a special rain. Instead of water, I sprayed a special kind of oil that fuels the fire to burn even more intensely." Hanuman was so satisfied with the assistance provided by the *deva*s in the mission of Lord Rama. Indra disappeared as quickly as he appeared, leaving behind a smiling Hanuman.

Observations from the Burning of Lanka

1. Ravana felt that *vanara*s were attached to their tails; therefore, Hanuman's attachment should be burned. Hanuman felt that by that logic, Lanka was Ravana's attachment; therefore, it had to be burned down.
2. Hanuman thought that his real attachment was to the limitless Rama. Ravana's attachment was to the limited Lanka. What is limited remains for short time; therefore, the glory of the limited Lanka was also limited.
3. Ravana believed that all demigods were under his command. He gloated about the complete control that he had on all the elements of nature including, fire, air and water. Hanuman wanted Ravana to know who their real master was; therefore, he burned Lanka.
4. Rama had sent Hanuman as a doctor to cure the sickness of Ravana. But when Ravana refused to take the doctor's advice,

Hanuman had to administer a medicine that required residual ash from gold and precious stones (as per Ayurveda). Thus Hanuman burned the golden city to procure the ash to cure Ravana of his disease of lust and attachments.

5. There was such a contrast between the way Ravana and Hanuman operated. When Ravana went to kidnap Sita, he made sure Rama wasn't there to protect Her. This was an exhibition of cowardice. But Hanuman exhibited great courage by attacking the city right in the presence of Ravana and Indrajit. Indrajit, who had launched *Brahma pasha* to restrain Hanuman, did not even try launching the Varunastra weapon to restrain the fire because he knew that this fire was beyond restraint.
6. Fire burned everything in Lanka except Vibhishan's house and Hanuman's tail. This shows that even fire has consciousness. Within everything in this world, there is divine consciousness. Great people learn to see divinity even within matter.

Suddenly that happy smile turned into a worried frown. *What have I done?* Only when the excitement was over and the adrenaline rush had waned did he realize his grave mistake. In a fit of anger, he had committed the biggest foolishness of his life. He began to curse himself for losing his sense of discrimination by being carried away by a spell of great anger. He felt miserable for becoming such a slave of wrath. He felt totally responsible for this grave mistake. Unwittingly, he had burned the entire Lanka without ensuring Sita's safety. He couldn't see a single part of Lanka that wasn't smoldering in the heat. Now that the whole city burned indiscriminately, he had no idea if Sita was at all safe. All his efforts of meeting Her and giving Her Rama's message would go in vain if She wasn't alive. For the first time in his life, he felt that he had acted like a *vanara*. He began to curse himself thinking that despite being so wise and well trained, he had acted so irrationally and had spoilt the purpose for which his Master had sent him. *How will I face Lord Rama and Sugriva now? What will I tell my friends who are eagerly waiting for me across the ocean? What a shame!* [7]

goodbye before another hello

Just as he was sulking, a thought struck him that changed his perspective. *How did the fire not burn me?* Not even a single hair on his skin was burned. In fact, he had felt extremely cool, as if a pack of ice had been applied to his tail when burning all over. *If it weren't for the grace of Mother Sita and the blessings of Lord Rama, how could I have survived that intense fire ordeal?* Hanuman reasoned that if he wasn't burned by the fire then Sita, too, would be unaffected by it. If by Her blessings, he had remained unscathed, She was unlikely to succumb to those very flames. His thought was confirmed by the auspicious omens around him. He decided to reconfirm it by paying a visit to Sita.[8]

In a moment, he landed in Ashoka *vatika*. He ambled unobstructed toward the *simshupa* tree under which he had last seen Sita. With

---

[7] The highest mistakes of life are those made during the highest peaks of excitement.

When filled with anger, even if one has knowledge, it is useless.

[8] Blessings are like a coating of alum that prevents one from being charred by the fiery elements of this world.

Her eyes closed and palms folded, Sita was seated in a lotus posture with an erect back offering prayer. As he approached Her, he could hear Her heartfelt prayers for his safety. He was touched by the mother's care and affection toward him. He once again assumed his small size. In front of Mother Sita, he couldn't exhibit any form other than that of a tiny *vanara* whom She could identify as Her son. When She realized that She wasn't alone, Sita opened Her eyes to see Hanuman offering his obeisance to Her. She was delighted to see him safe. She appreciated his boldness and intelligence in executing his mission. She praised his sharp wit in teaching Ravana and the entire *rakshasa* community a bit of humility by shattering the misconception of their invincibility. Once again Sita reminded Hanuman about the one-month deadline that She would wait for Rama to come and take Her back. She reiterated that She could have returned with him and saved Herself so much trouble, but She chose to wait to give the credit and glory to Lord Rama and help save the countless women in Ravana's captivity in Lanka.[9]

Reassuring Her that soon She would find the entire *vanara* army headed by Sugriva in Lanka and comforting Her that Rama would save Her from Ravana, Hanuman offered his obeisance to Her and jumped away from Ashoka *vatika.* He landed on the Arishta mountain on the farthest edge of Lanka jutting out into the ocean.[10]

---

[9] Humility allows one to learn even after one has grown up.

[10] When the *rakshasis* informed Sita about Hanuman's plight, She was pained. She began to pray to Agni to ensure that the flames did not harm Hanuman. As a result, not a single strand of hair on Hanuman's body was touched. If Sita had such command over fire, surely her threat to Ravana that She could reduce him to ashes by Her purity was also true. But She never used Her powers to protect Herself. Rather, she allowed Rama to exhibit His greatness by coming to save Her. That is Her greatness.

Mount Arishta was extremely beautiful and scenic. It was carpeted with lush grass everywhere and inhabited by the most majestic red-spotted elephants. Jutting out into the sea was a plateau on which Hanuman landed. The tabletop mountain extended right into the ocean ending at a vertical cliff that dropped right into the depths of the ocean floor. As Hanuman saw the ocean extend in front of him like a blue carpet, he felt excited. He was finally going to see Lord Rama once again. He was going to be reunited with his friends. His excitement reflected in his powerful strides as he ran at a great pace toward the edge of the mountain to take off on a yet another historic jump across the ocean. As he came closer to the edge, he began to increase in size. When he made his final leap in the northern direction, the southern winds blew from behind, propelling him on his flight. When his enlarged body took off from the mountain, it had a more drastic effect on the Arishta mountain than his take-off had on Mahendra mountain. The Arishta mountain experienced tremors, sank into the earth and ceased to exist.

CHAPTER 8

GOOD NEWS, BAD NEWS

back with friends

Hanuman's colossal body glided through the sky, appearing to swallow it up with his sheer size. He seemed to drag the clouds and scratch the moon. Tinged by the color of his body, the sky appeared reddish brown. Traversing at such heights he was sometimes visible and sometimes not, lost among the clouds. Clad in white apparel, Hanuman shone like the moon in broad daylight. Hanuman's occasional happy roars sounded like thunderclaps. His large silhouette on the ocean scared the big fishes and sea snakes to dive deeper, for they mistook it to be the shadow of their enemy Garuda, the king of eagles.[1]

As he reached midway, Mount Mainak's peak was still on the ocean surface. He had been patiently waiting for Hanuman all this while. On seeing his determination and desire to serve, Hanuman reduced his speed and touched the mountain, accepting all the hospitality

[1] A sense of achievement radiates in one's posture as confidence.

in his heart. Of course, by then Mainak had understood that the servant of Rama had no time to rest. From thereon, Hanuman was on the last phase of his journey. He would soon be reunited with his *vanara* friends who were eagerly waiting for his return. His intermittent fierce roars sent happiness waves through the skies, reflecting the joy he felt in his heart just thinking about them.[2]

When that roar reverberated and fell on the ears of the *vanara*s waiting by the ocean, they rejoiced. They had not even seen Hanuman, but his roars were indicators enough. As they looked up, they thought the sky would crack open with the sheer intensity of Hanuman's roars. For these *vanara*s who had been patiently waiting, looking at the empty skies for almost two days, the roars gave the same joy a thunderclap would give a farmer awaiting rain. Even before they could see their friend, their hearts began to dance in celebration.

The wise Jambavan spoke first. "This has to be the sound of victory. I am sure he has met Mother Sita in Lanka. If he hadn't, his roar couldn't have been so boisterous."[3]

On hearing their leader vocalize what was on their minds, the *vanara*s could not contain their happiness. Some were so excited that they climbed tall trees and mountain cliffs for a closer view of the sky. As they looked up, they saw two powerful hands split a large cloud. Those on the trees grasped the branches and shook

---

[2] Internal warmth does not come with external fires but with heat generated by a fiery mission. Such a fired-up missionary can never find time to rest.

[3] The peacock sounds happiest when it spots a cloud. One may not be able to experience the happiness of another, but one can surely hear the happiness of another when it bursts out through their voices.

them intensely, forcing a leaf shower. Those on the cliffs began to hoot and scream. The *vanaras* below joined their palms to welcome their hero when they heard the celebrations uphill and on trees.[4]

Hanuman landed on the Mahendra mountain very gracefully. He had taken off from the exact place two days ago. All the *vanaras* were very excited so they all climbed the peak to welcome Hanuman. They plucked fruits and roots along the way until they reached the spot their hero was seated. By now, Hanuman had reduced himself to his regular size. He was waiting for his friends to join him. As soon as Jambavan and Angad appeared, Hanuman stood up and offered his respects to his leaders. Jambavan stood up and embraced him to garland him and shower him with words of appreciation. When Hanuman announced he had met Sita, all the *vanaras* began to celebrate. Some roared, some lifted their tails and danced, some began to sing and yet others played the drums.

Once the excitement abated and peace returned, Hanuman narrated how the sequence of exciting events panned out in Lanka. He shared with them the sorrowful plight of Sita, who was trapped amid seven hundred horrifying *rakshasi* women. As Hanuman continued to describe Mother Sita's situation, all those seated around him began to cry. Just as they were touched by Sita's determination, they were euphoric about Hanuman's courage, devotion, wit and humility. The hospitality proposal of the golden mountain and the hundred-*yojana* of the wide-mouthed Surasa astonished them. The *vanaras* were relieved to hear the end of the shadow-grabbing demoness. They were awed by Lanka's opulence, irritated by the harassment

---

[4] Heroes have their feet on the ground with commoners, their head in the sky with the gods and their hearts deeply soaked in their mission. As far as their egos are concerned, there is no space to carry it around.

of the *rakshasis* and angered by Ravana's arrogance and pride. They thought Trijata's prophecy was ingenious. Vibhishan's saintliness excited them, Lanka's destruction thrilled them and the twenty-nine-day deadline made them anxious. They were confident about Rama's greatness and eager for a good fight!

The young prince Angad thought it better not to return to Kishkinda but venture together to Lanka and bring Sita along. He believed it was pointless to return with only a message from Sita and leave the task of bringing back Sita to Lord Rama. The wise Jambavan pacified the prince. "It is important that we respect Sita's choice. It doesn't matter what we think; it's about what Sita feels is right. We aren't deciding about our lives here. It's Her life. So the decision is Her's alone to make." Angad could see Jambavan's point and agreed to follow the group's decision. Time was crucial, so the *vanaras* decided to move to Kishkinda as soon as possible. A lot had to be done.[5]

What had earlier taken the *vanaras* two months to traverse took them only two days this time around. When they had traveled southward, they were searching for Sita and had to look in every direction carefully before proceeding. But now as they were returning from the south, they were not looking for anyone but looking forward to returning home instead. Besides, their hearts were no longer heavy and weighing them down. This time, the good news had put an extra spring in their steps.[6]

---

[5] By respecting someone's choices, one is respecting that person's freedom to choose.

[6] As much as excitement makes one run externally, anxiety makes one run internally on the treadmill of the mind.

sugriva's garden

By the time they reached the borders of the kingdom of Kishkinda, they were tired. They had neither rested for a single minute while covering hundreds of miles nor stopped to eat or drink. On entering Kishkinda, an intense fragrance assaulted their senses. Soon their stomachs began to growl. One of the *vanaras*, who was particularly hungry, approached prince Angad with a request. As fate would have it, they were near the entrance of Madhuvana, Sugriva's favorite and most exquisite garden. Although the *vanara* knew of its importance to Sugriva and that the king would never allow anyone entry or permission to see it, he was still tempted to taste a little honey from the garden. The smell of honey was too tempting for everyone. Angad's mouth was watering, too, but he felt it inappropriate to enter the king's garden without his permission.

The hungry *vanara* began to plead with Angad to allow him just ten minutes' break before proceeding. Angad wasn't adamant, so Jambavan stepped in to break the impasse. He noticed that everyone was famished. The last two months hadn't been easy on any one and neither would the next month. He felt that this was the last chance for the *vanara* army to get a deserving break, indulge a bit and relax their weary minds and body. He smiled at Angad, patted him on his back and dragged him toward the Madhuvana gardens. The *vanaras* were elated. They began to swoop into the gardens. The gates were locked and guarded, but the excited *vanaras* hardly bothered to take the normal route. They jumped over the wall and flooded the celebrated garden. When the guards responsible for the security of the garden noticed the mass infiltration, they ran to the chief guard Dadhimukha, who was quite taken aback by the invasion![7]

Thousands of *vanara*s were atop various trees. In fact, thousands had climbed every single tree. The *vanara*s were on a rampage, throwing down fruits, breaking honeycombs and trampling over flower gardens. There was such excitement. However, Dadhimukha thought this was in excess so he started warning some junior *vanaras*. When they pretended not to hear, he shoved them and pulled them off the trees and threw them aside. This annoyed the reveling *vanaras*. A whole gang jumped on him and thrashed him. Dadhimukha was outnumbered, but he wriggled out in time to save himself. Seeing their chief injured and not hopeful of being saved, the other guards ran away.[8]

Once the obstacles were taken care of, the *vanara*s began to relish their nectar. Soon each had huge quantities of honey in both their hands. The *vanara*s reveled in each other's company, indulged in all the honey and fruits they could, sang and danced. Some laughed hysterically from intoxication, some rolled on the ground while some others walked sideways. Some even blabbered in languages they did not know. Some were very quiet and only leaned on others. Some jumped from tree to tree endlessly, while some others kept falling from treetops. The *vanara*s had gone berserk and completely lost their senses. Not one *vanara* in that troop was sober.

---

[7] When an intense peak performance is followed by sensitive care, a powerful leader is blessed with loyal followers.

[8] Dadhimukha was chosen to be the guard because he loved curd and had no taste for fruits and honey; thus, Madhuvana was safe in his custody.

Responsibilities should be allotted not according to need-based choices but inclination-based tastes.

hope revived

Meanwhile, Dadhimukha fell at the feet of King Sugriva. When Sugriva saw one of his most trusted servants in a state of complete despair and all bruised, he assumed there was an emergency in the kingdom. But on careful consideration, Sugriva began to think. *Dadhimukha has no role in the kingdom's administration nor is he in the army. His job is to oversee a garden in Kishkinda, so how much of an emergency could there be in a garden?* Dadhimukha explained about the *vanara* crisis in Madhuvana. On hearing the whole narrative, Sugriva laughed out loud. Dadhimukha wasn't expecting this reaction at all. *Isn't he supposed to be angry that his favorite garden where even his friends are not allowed was ransacked by a group of unruly vanara soldiers?* Sugriva cleared the air for the confused Dadhimukha.

"When *vanaras* are very happy, they do destroy things. Don't worry, the *vanaras* who have entered the garden are led by Angad, Jambavan and Hanuman. The deadline to return was a month ago, but they have far surpassed that. However, despite disobedience at several levels, if they were cheeky enough to enter my favorite garden and damage it completely, it only means they are happy about something. What else could that happiness mean other than the good news that they have found Sita?" Sugriva then picked up a trembling Dadhimuka and gently patted his back. "Go back and summon the *vanaras* to the Malyavanta mountains. Tell them that I am neither upset nor worried about the garden."

Gardens of Joy and Sorrow

Ashoka *vatika* was Ravana's favorite garden and Madhuvana was Sugriva's favorite garden. Hanuman destroyed Ashoka *vatika* and all the *vanaras* together destroyed Madhuvana. If destroying Ashoka *vatika* brought so much unhappiness to Ravana, then destruction of Madhuvana should have made Sugriva equally unhappy. But rather than being unhappy, Sugriva was happy about the destruction of the garden because his joy was connected to Rama's joy. Hanuman's similar actions brought Ravana sorrow but Sugriva joy. This means that Hanuman's actions brought sorrow to evil people and joy to divine people.

As soon as Dadhimukha left, Sugriva rushed to share the good news with Lord Rama and Lakshmana who had been waiting patiently for the last two months without any contact or information from the last search party that had left southward in search for Sita.[9]

Every other search party had returned with news of failure despite having searched very nook. Sita's whereabouts had been unknown. Disappointed and dejected, they had all returned to an even more grief-stricken Rama. Hope seemed to have eluded Him this far. However, until the one person Lord Rama trusted the most in

[9] Sugriva tells Dadhimukha that Angad had every right to destroy Madhuvana because he was the crown prince and that he was only enjoying his father's property. Dadhimukha felt bad that he had even questioned Angad for entering the garden without the king's permission. He sought forgiveness from Angad who forgave him because he was happy from drinking all that honey.

the *vanara* army – Hanuman – had not given up hope, Rama was hopeful. It had been more than two months now and there had been no news from or about the southern team. So, Rama's hope had almost waned, and it had become dimmer with every passing day.[10]

[10] One cannot be the source of hope all the time. Even the sun must set to allow the moon to rise. Everyone needs a source of hope. One must be the source of hope to someone and must have a source of hope for oneself.

CHAPTER 9

BEGINNING OF THE END

joy to rama

Sugriva reached the summit of the Malyavanta mountain where Rama was stationed with His brother Lakshmana in a cave. Pandemonium seemed to have accompanied Sugriva, for just as he reached, he saw hordes of noisy and boisterous *vanaras* approaching from the southern direction. Right in the middle of the large army was Hanuman. Lord Rama's eagerness and anxiety intensified as He watched the last unit of the *vanara* army return. He was unsure of the news He would hear from them. Rama was under pressure as the *vanaras* were still some distance away for Him, and He did not know exactly what news was coming His way. Suddenly, He heard something. As soon as He heard those words, Rama was convinced that Hanuman was not only intelligent but also sensitive. He had conveyed his message to Rama in incorrect grammar to ensure the key words reached Him first.

"Found Sita I!" Hanuman had screamed from a distance.

Hanuman realized that the lack of any information about the

search operation must have put his master, Lord Rama, under tremendous pressure. He knew the failure of the leaders of the other search parties, who were now gathered around Lord Rama, had disappointed Him. He realized yet again, as he had in Lanka before communicating with Sita, that only the right choice of words would bring Rama comfort. He understood that saying "I found Sita" would put the word "I" first. After the repeated failure of various troops, it was quite likely that Lord Rama would assume that the "I" would be followed by "I did not find Sita". Just the thought might cause His instant death. Hanuman also ruled out announcing, "Sita I found," for even that could lead Lord Rama to arrive at the wrong conclusion. He might collapse or die assuming that Sita had perished.

The only word that would revive Lord Rama's hope and give Him the impetus to hold on until Hanuman reached Him was the word "found." That word was the sweetest to Rama's ears. The grammar was wrong, but the sensitivity was perfect. By distorting grammar, Hanuman had given Lord Rama's morale a boost for a few moments until they met and details followed.[1]

home, at last!

The southern search party, led by Angad and Hanuman, finally returned. The happy *vanaras* were darting ahead at great speed like

---

[1] Communication is not about perfection in grammar but about perfection in the ability to convey what a person wants to hear in a way that is sensitive and pleasant. Communication is about knowing and understanding the impact of spoken words.

stones from a catapult. Hanuman bent his head low and touched Lord Rama's feet and offered his deepest respects. Rama and Lakshmana had tears of joy in their eyes, tears that were flowing like water from a burst dam. All that pent-up anxiety was finally released. After almost ten months of absolutely no news, someone had something really good to convey. After offering his obeisance to Rama, Hanuman turned toward the south, lay down with his hands above his head and surrendered himself in prayer. When Rama saw the respect and worship Hanuman was offering even to the direction Sita was in, He became extremely happy.

All the *vanaras* stepped in and began to narrate all the incidents that took place in Lanka. They rattled on about the obstacles along their route until reaching south, the complications in crossing the ocean, the killing of so many demons, the challenges in Lanka, the destruction of Ashoka *vatika*, the burning of Lanka, the seven hundred *rakshasis* harassing Sita and Ravana's two-month deadline. The narrations were so intense, almost as if each had a part to play in all these events when none had even crossed the ocean. They all spoke so fast and out of turn that it was now a mishmash of information that was impossible to process. Although Rama heard them patiently, He wasn't really interested in hearing all that. Hanuman hadn't spoken at all about any of the events related to his Lankan adventure. He assessed Rama's mood and waited for Him to ask Him the most burning question in His heart.[2]

---

[2] The other *vanaras* had done nothing they were talking about, but they spoke as if they were part of all the action. They hadn't even crossed the ocean, let alone seeing Sita or destroying Ashok *vatika* or burning Lanka. The advantage of being a follower is that one can share the glory of the achievements of the leader. By following Hanuman, all the other monkeys became qualified to share their stories with Rama. On their own merit, there was hardly a chance of any of them interacting with Rama.

Once everyone had spoken and there was silence, Rama asked with tears of anguish in His eyes, "Is Sita alive?"

Everyone was bewildered by Rama's question. Everyone except Hanuman. After meeting Sita, He had understood the love between Rama and Sita. When Rama was leaving Ayodhya on exile, He didn't want to take Sita along. Sita had insisted that if She were to be separated from Him, She would die. Her words had kept ringing in Rama's mind all these months, so all He wanted to know was whether She had survived the separation.[3]

Hanuman said, "Mother Sita is eagerly waiting to leave Her body in separation from You, my dear Lord. But Her soul doesn't depart for a reason. A guard is blocking the exit door, and that protector is Your name. Sita's constant chant of Your various names doesn't allow Her to quit Her body. She is not concerned with anything external. Her focus is like a lock that has kept Her secure because of Her meditation and immersion in You. Your names and memories are saving Her from death.

Mother Sita asked me to convey that Her body is like cotton, which when kept close to fire in a windy environment can avoid being burned. Separation from You is like a fire. Her deep breathing in separation is like the wind that should have fanned the flames and Her body, but this separation is also creating an intense desire in Her to see You. This is pouring out of Her eyes like torrents to extinguish the fire of separation. I believe those tears are Your grace protecting Mother Sita's body from being burned down by the fire of separation. Her eyes are yearning for a glimpse of You. She is waiting impatiently for Your arrival."

[3] The depth of a person can be understood by the depth of the questions one poses.

DOUBLE NARRATION

In the *Sundara Kanda*, the narration of the events related to Hanuman's Lanka travel takes place twice. The first time Hanuman narrates it to the *vanara* army, and the second time Hanuman narrates it to Rama. On both occasions, Hanuman's narrative is different. When he speaks to the *vanaras*, he talks about all his exploits starting from Mainak all the way until the burning of Lanka but mentions nothing about his discussion with Sita. On the other hand, when he speaks to Rama, he doesn't mention anything about his exploits and only focuses on his conversation with Sita in detail because those details were meant only for Rama. While news about Sita made Rama happy, news about his feats thrilled the *vanaras*. He chose to omit any talk about his exploits to Rama out of humility. This shows Hanuman's discretion in speech. He knows whom to speak to, what to speak, how to speak and how much to speak.

wordly wise

At the first meeting itself Rama had realized that Hanuman was very wealthy. His wealth was his choice of words. Whenever and wherever he spoke, he simply touched listeners' hearts. Rama was so touched by Hanuman's reply to his first question that He wanted to ask more. Rama next asked him, "Where is My Sita?"

HATRED AND LOVE

There is a distinct difference between the reporting methods of Manthara and Hanuman.

In the beginning of the *Ramayana* when Manthara reports about Dasaratha's decision to Keikeyi, she does so in a way that the information causes hatred and negativity in Keikeyi. When Hanuman reports about Sita, he does so in a way that the information evokes a great surge of love and unites Rama with Sita even more.

Merely reporting the truth is not enough. It is more important to know how that truth will impact the receiver of the report. Manthara was proud that of all the citizens of Ayodhya, she was the only one with the guts to speak the truth. But her perceived truth created hatred amid people who loved each other and caused a national disturbance. Manthara was an expert in the art of manipulating words, Hanuman is an expert in nurturing words. While Manthara's expertise divided people, Hanuman's expertise united two parted souls. It's not enough to wear a blanket of pride for speaking the truth, it is important to be sensitive enough to gauge the impact of the truth.

Hanuman continued his narration. "Right in the middle of the southern ocean is an island called Lanka. Right in the middle of Lanka is a garden called Ashoka *vatika*. Right in the middle of that garden is a large circle of seven hundred *rakshasis*. Right in the middle of that large circle of *rakshasis* is a beautiful golden *simshupa* tree. Right under that simshupa tree is Mother Sita with two flowers on either side. While one represents Rama and the other is

Lakshmana. Sita sits under the tree and cries for Her beloved Lord Rama. The Sita who had a more prosperous existence than Lakshmi herself now lives in grief. She looks emaciated and miserable, and Her hair is always in a single plait. She is determined not to succumb to Ravana but is vulnerable to the wounds of separation from You. When I offered Her Your ring, She was thrilled and excited. She clutched the ring as if She were holding Your handsome face in Her palms.

Rama's Ring

The ring that Rama gave Hanuman to carry had His holy name inscribed in it. Hanuman carried the ring in his mouth implying that the holy name of Lord Rama should always be in one's mouth.

When Hanuman saw Mother Sita in the Ashoka *vatika*, she had been praying to the Ashoka trees to help Her become *ashoka* or free from lamentation (*shoka*). When Hanuman gave Her the ring, he told Her that only Lord Rama's holy names could help Her become free from lamentation.

Hanuman told Her that Rama's name has three syllables. Ra, which represented *agni* or fire, Aa, which represented *chandra* or moon and *Ma* which represented *surya* or the sun. It means that in the scorching heat of lamentation, Rama's name would give the coolness of the moon. In the darkness of lamentation, Rama's name would offer the brightness of the sun. As far as the fire element in Rama's name was concerned, Hanuman decided to use that to burn Lanka, which represented all material attachments that prevent one from chanting Rama's name.

She sent You a gift that will serve both as tangible proof that I met Her and as a loving memory of Her since this was Her only companion for the ten long months of separation. She also told me several very intimate stories that only the two of You would know."

Hanuman narrated each event in detail. Finally, he brought out the *chudamani* Sita had given him and gave it to a teary-eyed Rama. Memories of His beloved came flooding back to Him, and He couldn't be the sober, controlled leader anymore. He broke down. The entire *vanara* army assembled around the Lord also wept on seeing the plight of the person they loved so dearly. To lighten the mood, Hanuman narrated the episode of *kakasura* that Mother Sita had shared with him. On seeing Sita's *chudamani* and hearing the story of *kakasura*, Lord Rama knew beyond doubt that Hanuman had indeed met Her. Hanuman shared with Rama that after narrating this story, Sita had asked him why Rama had not sent a similar *astra* this time to save Her from a more dangerous demon?

Of course, Hanuman did not expect an answer to this question from Rama, so he continued with his story and shared the discussion he had with Sita. He then told Rama about Sita's doubt if the *vanara* army could cross the huge ocean. He went on to explain how he had told Her that if the most mediocre messenger from the army could cross the ocean in one leap, the more competent ones would easily be able to do it. Rama smiled at Hanuman's modesty. Finally, Hanuman spoke about Sita's reasons for refusing to come with him into the loving embrace of Rama in Kishkinda, away from the clutches of Ravana.

Of all the various reasons that Sita gave for refusing to come with Hanuman, when Rama heard Her final reason of wanting the glory of Her rescue to go only to Her husband, He burst into tears. Even amid such trouble and inconveniences, Sita was worried about His reputation and glory. Rama was touched by Sita's greatness and purity.

Suddenly Rama's facial expression changed, and He seemed upset about something. He looked at Hanuman and asked him a very unexpected question. He said, "But why did you burn Lanka? That was not Our plan. When you had simply gone to search for Sita and give Her a message, what was the need to burn down the city?"

Hanuman smiled. His first words of clarification behind his mysterious smile bewildered Rama, "I burned Lanka because You made me burn it." "How could I make you burn Lanka when I wasn't even there?" Rama waited for Hanuman's explanation.

"After I spoke to Mother Sita, my mission was complete. But I had a doubt if my mission was complete. This was because I heard Trijata, one of the *rakshasis* in Ashoka *vatika*, narrate her dream to Sita. In her dream, she had seen a *vanara* burn Lanka. I wondered if that was Your will for me spoken through the mouth of a *rakshasi*. I decided that the only way I would know what You wanted me to do was if I didn't have the freedom to choose from many options. If I have the freedom to choose, then it would be my desire. But if I have no freedom to choose then whatever happens is the will of Lord Rama. Thus, I allowed Indrajit to tie me to up with the *Brahma pasha*. Once I was tied, I began to pray for direction. Just then Ravana, influenced by the divine will of Rama, had this brilliant idea of burning my tail. Ravana could have easily done anything else like cutting it off or stabbing me. Why did he choose to burn my tail? Who influenced him to think about it if not the *paramatma* or the voice of God from within his heart? The moment Ravana began to order his people to get cloth, oil and torches, I realized that it was Your will to use Ravana's organizational skills to burn his own city. Once I realized that You were providing me with all the ingredients through Ravana, I was sure that it was Your will. How else would I have got all those ingredients necessary to start such a major fire in Lanka?"

Hanuman's logic and justification captivated the *vanaras*. That was deep thinking indeed. Rama was impressed with Hanuman, too, not only for his strength but also his wisdom, commitment, sensitivity, achievements and deep devotion. Rama stood up and expressed His gratitude to Hanuman for having taken the trouble of finding Sita. He told him that both He and the entire Raghu dynasty were grateful for his heroic acts.[4]

Rama continued speaking gracefully. "O Hanuman, I do not have anything valuable to offer you in appreciation of your tremendous service. For all that you have done for Me, I have only My loving embrace to offer. Please accept it as My all."

Rama pulled Hanuman closer to His heart and embraced him lovingly. In the warmth of that embrace, Lord Hanuman melted inside. He closed his eyes and savored every moment of that embrace. He wanted the memory of this embrace to remain in his subconscious forever. He considered himself fortunate enough to receive the embrace great sages hankered for after performing severe penances for thousands of years. Hanuman thought there was nothing more valuable than this that Lord Rama could have ever offered him. With that embrace, Hanuman got the inspiration to dedicate his life to Lord Rama's service and a desire to please Him in every possible way. He decided that his life's aspiration was to receive another embrace from Lord Rama.

---

[4] Calling Hanuman His son, Rama said that generally a son owes his parents a debt for his upbringing. But Hanuman was a son who made his parents indebted. With tears of gratitude, Rama explained to Hanuman that He had no difficulty raising this son, but the son had to go through so many difficulties for the sake of uniting his parents. Rama explained that Hanuman had turned the parent–child relationship on its head. Generally, a father carries the son, but here the son was carrying the father.

Five Blessings

When Hanuman met Mother Sita at Ashoka *vatika*, She gave him five blessings. She offered him complete strength, calmness, eternity, immortality and virtues. While She was offering these five boons, Hanuman remained silent. But as soon as Sita offered Her sixth boon, Hanuman spoke up. She was surprised by his silence earlier and this sudden waking up.

Hanuman replied that Her first five boons were like the five elements of creation. He was in the process of taking re-birth. The sixth boon that She offered was like life-air entering the body. As soon as life entered, he began to speak. And what was Sita's sixth boon that made Hanuman alive and so eager to speak? That Rama would always love him. That boon gave life to Hanuman.

The next thing that Hanuman did was to ask Sita for something to eat as he was hungry. Once a child is born, the first thing it needs is nourishment from the mother. Now that he was re-born as the son of Sita, She had to feed him now. Sita offered Hanuman fruits to satisfy his hunger. This was not the hunger of the belly but that of the soul to experience love from the divine mother.

During Rama's embrace, Hanuman expressed his gratitude mentally to Mother Sita because of whose sixth boon Rama had actually begun to love Hanuman. Before Hanuman left on the search mission, Rama had hardly spoken much to him. But when he came back, there was a very different dynamism in their relationship because of the grace of Sita. One's connection with the divine father is firmly established because of the grace of the divine mother.

call to action

When the warmth of that embrace was over, the calamitous reality of the present dawned on him. Holding the hands of Lord Rama, Hanuman revealed Sita's final parting instruction. "Mother Sita has given us a one-month deadline to claim Her back from Lanka, failing which She would end Her life. She told me to tell You that She considers You to be *deenadayaal* or the most compassionate one. At this point, She has given You one month to show Your compassion to Her. Since the day She uttered this, three days have passed. We only have twenty-seven days left now before we lose Her forever."

When Rama heard of the time limit set by Sita, He sprang into action. Sita's words conveyed through Hanuman's mouth seemed to be a catalyst that charged Rama. Standing upon a rock on the Malyavanta mountain, Lord Rama pointed to the southern direction and looked at Sugriva. At the top of his voice with all the energy he could muster, Sugriva delivered his command.

"TO THE SOUTHHHHH!"

The earth began to vibrate suddenly. The *vanara*s had placed their first step toward the south amid cracking stones and mountains.

THE SPECIALTY OF *SUNDARA KANDA*

The *Sundara Kanda* is special for many reasons

1. This *kanda* talks about the beauty of neither Rama nor Sita but of Hanuman. A *vanara* is never considered beautiful, but Hanuman is considered the most beautiful purely because of

his utmost devotion and service to Lord Rama. Not only his form, but his actions and speech are also beautiful.

2. Hanuman plays the role of a guru who acts as a go-between and unites the living entity with God by offering hope.

3. Hanuman is transformed from being Rama *doota* to Rama *dasa* by the grace of Mother Sita.

4. This *kanda* reveals the greatness of Mother Sita and the power of Her purity, which is why Valmiki refers to the *Ramayana* as *Seetaayah charitam mahat* or the book that extols the virtues of Sita.

5. This is an all-encompassing *kanda* in that all other preceding *kandas* of the *Ramayana* are contained within it. This is because Hanuman narrates the entire *Ramayana* to Sita – from the beginning of *Bala Kanda* to *Kishkinda Kanda*. Reading the *Sundara Kanda* alone gives the benefit of reading the entire *Ramayana*.

6. Hanuman's journey to Lanka represents a *sadhaka*'s or a devotee's journey to *bhakti*. Sita represents *bhaktidevi* and Hanuman represents a *bhakta* in search of *bhakti*. By carefully observing his journey, one learns about the various obstacles one encounters in one's journey to find *bhakti*. Hanuman had to face demons, who symbolize the bad habits and negative thoughts that come as obstacles. This *kanda* makes an example of Hanuman to show one how to deal with each obstacle that one faces along the path of *bhakti*.

7. Hanuman is the perfect *yogi*, who uses *karma yoga*, *gyan yoga* and *bhakti yoga*, all to his advantage. As he performs his *seva* to his master Lord Rama, he uses various *yogas* at different times.

When he becomes massive and lightweight to burn the city of Lanka, he is a *karma yogi*. When he increases in size and weight to fight demons in the ocean and in Lanka, he is an expert *gyan yogi*. When he becomes tiny to enter Lanka, he does so as a *bhakti yogi*. When he makes himself extremely tiny in front of Mother Sita, it is a symbol of total surrender. Only Hanuman knows how to use the best of all avenues in the service of the Lord.

8. *Sundara Kanda* is about our purpose in life – our own search for a goal in life. Hanuman shows us that the goal of life is Sita, who he is searching for in this *kanda*. For a *gyani*, Sita is *shanti* or peace. For a devotee, Sita is *bhakti*. For a *yogi*, She is *adishakti* or subtle strength. The truth is that everyone is in search of Sita.

About the Author

Shubha Vilas is a TEDx speaker, lifestyle coach, storyteller, and author. He studied patent law after completing his engineering degree but, finally, chose the path of a spiritual seeker.

Ramayana: The Game of Life is his bestselling series. He is also the author of *Open-Eyed Meditations*, *Mystical Tales for a Magical Life* and *Perfect Love: 5.5 Ways to a Lasting Relationship*. The focus of his work is the application of scriptural wisdom in everyday living, addressing the needs of corporates and youth through thought-provoking seminars. He has delivered more than 4000 lectures worldwide and is a visiting faculty at the Indian Institute of Management.

To know more about him, visit www.shubhavilas.com.